PRAYERS
that avail much®

FOR GRADUATES

GERMAINE COPELAND

*This is the confidence we have before him: If we ask
anything according to his will, he hears us. And if we
know that he hears whatever we ask, we know that
we have what we have asked of him.*

1 John 5:14,15 (CSB)

Harrison House

Shippensburg, PA

Prayers That Avail Much® for Graduates is a collection of prayers and confessions from the following previously published Germaine Copeland books: *Prayers That Avail Much® for Young Adults, Prayers That Avail Much® for the College Years, Prayers That Avail Much® for the Workplace, and Prayers That Avail Much® for Leaders.*

Prayers that Avail Much® for Graduates
ISBN 978-1-68031-263-8
Ebook ISBN: 978-1-68031-264-5
1 2 3 4 5 6 7 8 / 23 22 21 20 19
Copyright © 2019 by Germaine Copeland
P.O. Box 310
Shippensburg, PA 17257-0310 www.harrisonhouse.com

Presented to:

Ashley Blocker

By:

The Lynch Family

Date:

May 11, 2019

Graduation from:

University of Georgia

Contents

Dedicated to

Chandler Grace Sutton, my granddaughter, who is a gifted poet and artist. She graduated from Westminster Christian Academy in 2016 and is currently exploring ways to use her God-given gifts to inspire others. She desires to bring comfort and consolation to those walking through the trials of life. This poem was penned during a difficult period when she was in high school. I had the honor of reading the following poem at her high school baccalaureate service.

Where I'm From

By: Chandler Grace Sutton

I am from written fantasies, liquid colors,
the bald headed man, who always wears white,
and paper given life using graphite.

I am from the brick house and pool on Beacon Way,
the red roof and many bike rides in Sandestin,
the murky waters of Lake Oconee, and the refreshing sea breeze.

I am from the grains of sand that get stuck between your toes,
the great oak that twisted and turned,
creating the perfect reading spot.
From the pink and yellow shades of Lantana that is always
in our front yard, no matter where we go.

I am from the chilly nights in the courtyard,
stargazing, and warming hot coco,
from days and days spent bathing in the warmth
of the sun on the dunes,
from cool mornings and enthusiastic parents at soccer games.

I am from Easter egg hunts and lemonade at grandmama's house,
from Lynn, Aunt T, David, and my beloved Beau.
From stubbornness, strength, pain, and suffering.

I am from love one another and broken promises,
from the temptations of the world, the loss of a father,
and the struggle to find one.

I am from Prayers That Avail Much, Sunday school, church hymns,
complete faith in God, and a beautiful example of his love.
I am from ashes and smoke stained walls, and endless prayer.

I am from southern belles and Georgia peaches,
bulldawgs, and Hosta bushes,
from accordance with the law and the strength of one woman.
From the salty and crunchy, hand-picked fried okra,
homemade blackberry jam,
and heavenly mashed potatoes.

I am from boxes of forgotten memories, a painful seven hours,
and the realization that I was loosing everything I loved .

I am from lost picture frames and emotional clutters
from magnolia trees, totem poles, my grandmama's playhouse,
and a closet full of comic books.

I am from late hours, deep conversations, and written fantasies.

Used by permission.

Introduction

CONGRATULATIONS! Graduation and years of study and academic preparation are behind you. What lies ahead? Only the rest of your life. You're standing at the threshold of your future where many of life's biggest decisions await you.

You matter to God, and He has plans for you! You are here because He has need of you, and He loves you. Knowing where you come from is a good beginning as you enter another season of life. God chose you before the foundation of the world, and He sees you as an eternal being.[1] He has a purpose for you, and as you renew your mind to the Word of God, His will for you becomes clear. There are many opportunities awaiting you, and you will have many choices to make because we need one another. We need builders, electricians, plumbers, service people, and housekeepers. We need counselors, educators, scientists, doctors, ministers, bankers, attorneys, entertainers, news reporters in print, television, and radio. We need writers, designers, and artists—and the list continues. Yes, we need one another!

You are a change agent for your generation. The choices that you make are vital, and the prayers in this book will assist you as you search for your answers. Read the scriptures listed at the end

1   Ecclesiastes 3:11

of each prayer. Do not skip over them because they are important. As you pray the prayer aloud, your mind will be renewed to the Word of God, and you will know God's will for you. He sent us a Teacher and Guide who knows all, and He is your constant companion. Realize that you are God's masterpiece.

You have faced challenges and learned more about life than you realize. As you begin another chapter in your book of life, remember God's eyes saw your unformed substance, and in His book He has written all the days of your life.[2] His plans for you are for good and to give you a hope and a future, so dare to dream big and dare to trust the One who knows you best and loves you most.

My prayer for you is that you will not "become so well-adjusted to your culture that you fit into it without even thinking. Instead, fix your attention on God. You'll be changed from the inside out. Readily recognize what he wants from you, and quickly respond to it. Unlike the culture around you, always dragging you down to its level of immaturity, God brings the best out of you, and develops well-formed maturity in you" (Romans 12:2 MSG).

The prayers in this book will help you focus and keep your eyes on the Author and Finisher of your faith. You have a large crowd of witnesses all around you, so get rid of everything that slows you down, especially the sin that just doesn't want to let go. God has

2   Psalm 139:16 (AMPC)

equipped you with power to overcome the evil one, and you are more than a conqueror through the One who loves you. With every temptation, your Father has made a way of escape and given you the power to choose love or fear. Choose love rather than fear and walk in the light of love rather than darkness! Treasure God's wisdom...then you will discover all that is just, proper, and fair, and be empowered to make the right decisions as you walk into your destiny.[3]

Let me offer you a few practical tips as well. Stay centered and well-balanced in an ever-changing world. As you pursue your dreams, these simple tools could prove helpful: 1) Be honest with yourself and with God. Speak truly, live truly, and deal truly with others. 2) Remain teachable, which is true humility. 3) Develop the practice of prayer. 4) Read the book of Proverbs. 5) Be kind to others. 6) Maintain an attitude of gratitude. 7) Visualize yourself ever learning, ever growing, and ever achieving to the glory and honor of God.

And remember, you have a friend praying for you!

—Germaine

---

3   Proverbs 2:1, 9 TPT

PART I:

The Me God Wants Me to Be

First Things First

FATHER, I thank You for choosing me before the foundation of the world and revealing to me who Jesus is. I confess with my mouth the Lord Jesus and believe in my heart that You raised Him from the dead. Jesus is my Lord, and I choose to believe that He will do what He said He will do. You rescued me from the power of darkness and drew me into the kingdom of the Son of Your Love. Your kingdom is in me. I am in Christ, and He is in me. My identity is in Him, the One who is transforming me into my true self—the child-of-God self. I love You because You first loved me, and with the help of the Holy Spirit, I choose to love others as I love myself. I long to know the wonders of Jesus more fully and to experience the overflowing power of His resurrection working in me. Grant me the discernment to make choices that will honor and glorify You. In Jesus' name I pray. Amen.

SCRIPTURE REFERENCES

Ephesians 1:4-5 NKJV

John 1:1-13 MSG

1 Corinthians 1:30 NJKV

John 13:34-35

Romans 10:9-10 NKJV

Colossians 1:13-14 AMPC

1 John 4:19

Philippians 3:13 TPT

Growing in Wisdom

FATHER, as I approach another important decision of study and/or career, I ask for the ability to understand words of insight and to understand biblical doctrine. I choose to be disciplined and wise in the management of those things that concern me and my future, so I will choose what is right and just and fair.

I ask for prudence, knowledge, and discretion. I seek, and I shall find. I knock, and doors will be opened. With Your help, I am becoming a wise person who is learning to listen so that I add to my learning. As a discerning person, I accept guidance [so I may be able to steer my course rightly].

I choose to read the Scriptures so that I understand proverbs and parables, the sayings and riddles of the wise. I choose to delight in the law of the Lord and meditate on it day and night. In a multitude of counselors there is safety. I look for and listen to wise counselors and submit myself to the constant ministry of transformation by the Holy Spirit. In Jesus' name I pray. Amen.

SCRIPTURE
REFERENCES

Proverbs 1:2-7 NIV   Proverbs 1:5 AMP

Psalm 1   2 Corinthians 3:18

Matthew 7:7-12

Who I Am in Christ

FATHER, thank You for sending the Holy Spirit, who teaches and leads me into all truth. Before I can truly know who I am, I must know You. You are infinite, and You are Love; I am born of Love. Today, I choose life and blessings, and I acknowledge that You qualified me and made me fit to share in the inheritance of Your Son. In You there is no darkness, and I am in the Light. I am in the world, but I am not of this world. My wrong perceptions are being cleansed with the water of the Word, and I am renewing my mind. Once I was blind, but now I can see even when I'm surrounded by darkness. I choose to walk in Love, in Light, and with a spirit of a sound, well-balanced mind. I am more than a conqueror in this life. I am who I am by the grace of God. In Jesus' name. Amen.

SCRIPTURE REFERENCES

John 16:13

1 John 4:8

Deuteronomy 30:19

1 John 1:5

Ephesians 5:26

John 9:25

Ephesians 5:1

1 John 4:7

Colossians 1:12 AMP

John 17:14

Romans 12:2

2 Timothy 1:7

Romans 8:37

Beginning Each Day

FATHER, today belongs to You! I will celebrate and be glad wherever I may be. You made all things by the power of Your Word, and You know all things. I begin my day trusting in You, and I choose to seek Your will in all that I do. When the time comes to make decisions, I believe You will show me which path to take.

I completely trust You and place myself and those for whom I pray in your keeping knowing You are able to guard everything and everyone I entrust to You. Thank You for ordering Your angels to protect me, my family, and friends. They will hold us up with their hands, so we won't even hurt our feet on a stone. Thank You, Father that Your love never ends, and Your mercy never stops. Your loyalty to me is awesome!

Father, I kneel in prayer to You. Thank You for generously giving me supernatural grace, according to the size of the gift of Christ who lives in me. This life that I live now, I live by faith in the Son of God, who loved me and gave his life for me. You can do anything, Father—far more than I could ever imagine or guess or request in my wildest dreams by Your Spirit within me. Glory to You forever! Amen.

SCRIPTURE REFERENCES

Psalm 118:24 CEV

John 1:1-3

Lamentations 3:22-23 NCV

Galatians 2:20 GNT

Psalm 143:8

Psalm 91:11-12 NLT

Ephesians 4:7 TPT

Ephesians 3:20 MSG

Son or Daughter of God

FATHER, I am amazed when I read that You knew me before time began. You fashioned me in the likeness of the image of Your Son. You, the Creator of the universe, called me and made me righteous, and You glorified me.

When I received Jesus and believed on His name, You gave me the right to become Your child. As He is so also I am in this world. I am a partaker of Your divine nature. Before You formed me in my mother's womb, You knew me. I am the light of the world. I believe that I am who You say I am, and I am free from the lies of the enemy.

I am Your child—an heir of God and a joint-heir with Christ. I rejoice, Father, because You have said that You will be a Father unto me and I shall be Your son/daughter.

Today I am Your child. You are the God who sees, the God who hears, and the God who watches over me.

SCRIPTURE REFERENCES

Romans 8:29-30   John 1:12-13

1 John 4:17   2 Peter 1:1-4

Jeremiah 1:5   John 1:15

1 Corinthians 6:16-17

Victorious over Fear

FATHER, Your Word is truth, and I choose not to let my heart be troubled. Along this journey there are storms and smooth seas, mountains and valleys, darkness and light, and at times I cannot see the path to walk. I sense fear, but when I feel afraid, I choose to put my confidence in You. Yes, I choose to trust Your promises.

You did not give me a spirit of timidity but of power and love and discipline (sound judgment). The Holy Spirit that You have given to me has flooded my heart with Your love. There is no fear in love; but perfect love casts out fear, because fear involves torment.

Jesus, You delivered me, who through fear of death had been living all my life as a slave to constant dread. I receive the gift You left to me—peace of mind and heart! And the peace You give isn't fragile like the peace the world gives. I take fearful thoughts captive and cast them far from me. I choose not to be afraid. I believe in God; I believe also in You.

Lord, You are my light and my salvation, You protect me from danger—whom shall I fear? When evil men come to destroy me, they will stumble and fall! Yes, though a mighty army marches against me, my heart shall not fear! I am confident that You will save me.

Thank You, Holy Spirit, for bringing these things to my remembrance when I am tempted to be afraid. I will trust in my God. In the name of Jesus, I pray.

SCRIPTURE REFERENCES

John 14:1 NKJV	John 17:17
Psalm 56:3-5 TLB	Hebrews 2:15 TLB
1 Timothy 1:7-8 NAS	John 14:1,17 TLB
Romans 8:15 NAS	Romans 5:5 Voice
1 John 4:18a NKJV	Psalm 27:1-3 TLB

Creative Words

Lord, let my words and my thoughts be pleasing to You because You are my mighty Rock and my Protector. My words contain the power to create, and I desire to speak words of life and blessings. I am Your masterpiece, and I desire to reflect Your glory and bring heaven to earth. Jesus taught me to pray, "Your Kingdom come; Your will be done on earth even as it is in heaven." I am spirit, soul, and body. I am unique, and with my mind I think, feel, and choose.

I choose to set my mind on things that are above where Christ is seated at Your right hand. I will meditate on whatever things are true, whatever things are noble, whatever things are just, whatever things are pure, whatever things are lovely, and whatever things are of good report. If there is any virtue and if there is anything praiseworthy—I choose to meditate on these things.

For the overflow of what has been stored in Your heart will be seen by my fruit and will be heard in my words. Out of my heart flow the issues of life.

In my conversations, I choose to speak truth with my neighbor because we are members of one another. I pray that the words I speak will be good for necessary edification, so they may impart grace to the hearers. In Jesus' name I pray. Amen.

SCRIPTURE REFERENCES

Psalm 19:14

Matthew 6:10

Colossians 3:1

Luke 6:45 TPT

Proverbs 18:21

1 Thessalonians 5:23

Philippians 4:8

Ephesians 4:25, 29

Overcoming the Fear of Rejection

FATHER forgive me for rejecting myself and allowing myself to feel unacceptable; forgive me for wishing I could be someone different. No longer will I live in fear of being rejected by others, but I will walk in the light because I am a child of the light, born of love. What I think and feel about myself matters because I am made in Your image. My body has been bought with a price, and I choose to glorify You with my spirit and body. You chose me, and I am accepted in Your Beloved. Jesus is my elder brother.

You are my Father, and I choose to present my body to You as a living sacrifice, holy and acceptable. I choose to walk in the light of Your acceptance rather than in fear of men and their opinions. I choose life and blessings. My birth was not a mistake. You chose me to be here on earth to honor and glorify You for Your good pleasure. You created me spirit, gave me an incredible mind, and gave me an amazing, complex body. Today, I will unlearn the fear of man's opinion by meditating on this acceptance by my God and Father. Christ is in me, and I am in Christ. We are one! Thank You, for choosing me to be Your very own child before You formed me in my mother's womb. You set me apart before the foundation of the world to go into all the world and make disciples, teaching them to observe all things that You have commanded me. You are always with me, even to the end of the age. Amen.

SCRIPTURE REFERENCES

1 Corinthians 6:20	2 Corinthians 10:2
Romans 12:1	Proverbs 29:25
Jeremiah 1:5 NKJV	Matthew 28:20 NKJV

Confident for Life

JEHOVAH God, I am Your child, and You are my Father. Because Your presence goes with me, I am ready to face each day with its new beginnings. Yesterday is gone. Old things have passed away; behold, all things have become new. Now all things are of You.

Once I was darkness, but now I am light. I live as a child of the light. The light produces in me all that is good and right and true. I desire for my life to be living proof of the things which please You. Light is capable of showing up everything for what it really is.

I will do all I have to do without grumbling or arguing, so I may be blameless and harmless, Your faultless child, living in a warped and diseased age, and shining like a light in a dark world.

You, Father, are the Vinedresser. Jesus is the Vine, and I am the branch. I am fruitful in all my work, for I share His life and He shares my life. You always cause me to triumph in Christ Jesus, in whose name I pray. Amen.

SCRIPTURE REFERENCES

1 Corinthians 5:17,18

John 15:1-7 NIV

Ephesians 5:8-11,13 Phillips

2 Corinthians 2:14

Philippians 2:14,15 Phillips

Overcoming Intimidation

FATHER, I come to You in the name of Jesus, confessing that intimidation has caused me to stumble. I ask Your forgiveness for thinking of myself as inferior, for I am created in Your image, and I am Your workmanship. Jesus said that Your kingdom is within me. Therefore, the power that raised Jesus from the dead dwells in me and causes me to face life with hope and divine energy.

You, Lord, are my light and my salvation; whom shall I fear? You are the strength of my life; of whom shall I be afraid?

Father, You have said that You will never leave me or forsake me.

Therefore, I can say without any doubt or fear that You are my Helper, and I am not afraid of anything that a mere human being can do to me. I am free from the fear of other people and the pressure of public opinion.

Father, You have given me a spirit of power and of love and of a calm and well-balanced mind of discipline and self-control.

Greater is He who is in me than he who is in the world. In all situations I remain calm, masterful, and at peace with God and who I am in Christ. If God be for me, who can be against me? In Jesus' name I pray. Amen.

SCRIPTURE REFERENCES

1 John 1:9

Hebrews 13:5,6

Genesis 1:27

1 John 4:4

Ephesians 2:10

Romans 8:31

2 Timothy 1:7 AMP

Ephesians 1:19,20

Philippians 4:13 NIV

Colossians 1:29

Proverbs 29:25

Psalm 27:1

Luke 17:21

Strong Self-Esteem

FATHER, I come to Your throne room to receive help for my self-image. You created me in Your image and likeness. I know that You always love me. I know You didn't just carelessly or thoughtlessly throw me together. You made me so wonderfully complex! It is amazing to think about. Your workmanship is marvelous—and how well I know it.

Because I am Your workmanship, Your handicraft made for good works, I ask You to help me to view myself from Your perspective. Help me to realize my strengths. Open my eyes to the strengths, abilities, and talents You have placed inside of me. Give me grace to find the good that is in me. Help me to be appreciative of who I am—instead of critical of who I am not.

Although the world places importance on physical appearance, Father, I know that You judge the heart. You are interested in a pure heart and a humble spirit. I know that I am very valuable to You. Knowing that I am chosen makes me feel special. Thank You for choosing me before the foundation of the world. I acknowledge You, God, as my Father. Thank You that I am Your child. I accept myself as You made me, and I am grateful for this body that You fashioned for me to live in here on earth.

Help me to set my affections on things above where Christ is seated at Your right hand rather than on things of the world. Help me to mature in my relationship with You and to develop into the happy, joyful, strong Christian I have the potential to be. In Jesus' name I pray. Amen.

SCRIPTURE REFERENCES

Genesis 1:27

1 Samuel 16:7

Psalm 139:14

Isaiah 57:15

Romans 12:1

Ephesians 1:4 KJV; 2:10 AMP

Colossians 3:2

Hebrews 4:16

1 Peter 2:9; 4:10

1 John 3:1-3

2 Corinthians 6:18

Walking in the Word

FATHER, in the name of Jesus, I choose to live in the Word and walk in its truth. Your Word living in me produces Your life in this world. I recognize that Your Word is integrity itself, and I trust my life to its provisions.

You have sent Your Word forth into my heart. It dwells in me richly in all wisdom. I meditate in it day and night so I may diligently act on it. The Incorruptible Seed is abiding in my spirit, growing mightily in me now, producing Your nature, Your life. It is my counsel, my shield, my buckler, my powerful weapon in battle.

The Word is a lamp to my feet and a light to my path, making my way plain before me. I do not stumble, for my steps are ordered in the Word.

The Holy Spirit leads and guides me into all the truth, giving me understanding, discernment, and comprehension so that I am preserved from the snares of the evil one.

I delight myself in You and Your Word, and You put Your desires within my heart. I commit my way unto You, and You make me successful. You are working in me now, giving me the power and desire to do all Your will. With all my heart, I rely on You to guide me and lead me in every decision I make.

I exalt Your Word, hold it in high esteem, and give it first place. I make my schedule around Your Word, making the Word the final authority to settle all questions that confront me. I agree with the Word of God, and disagree with any thoughts, attitudes, or circumstances contrary to Your Word. I boldly and confidently say that my heart is fixed and established on the solid foundation—the living Word of God!

SCRIPTURE REFERENCES

Psalms 37:4, 5, 23; 91:4; 112:7, 8; 119:1, 105

John 16:13

Ephesians 6:10

Hebrews 4:12

Luke 18:1

Colossians 1:9; 3:16; 4:2

Philippians 2:13

Joshua 1:8

2 Corinthians 10:5

1 Peter 1:23; 3:12

Proverbs 2:1b TPT

Obtaining and Maintaining Godly Character

FATHER, I desire to receive wisdom and discipline. I ask for the ability to understand words of insight. By Your grace, I am acquiring a disciplined and prudent life, doing what is right and just and fair.

Thank You for giving me prudence, knowledge, and discretion. As a wise person I listen and add to my learning, and as a discerning person I accept guidance [so that I may be able to steer my course rightly].

Thank You that I understand proverbs and parables, the sayings and riddles of the wise. In Jesus' name I pray. Amen.

SCRIPTURE REFERENCES

Proverbs 1:2-7 NIV

Proverbs 1:5 AMP

To Be Well-Balanced and Vigilant

FATHER, in the name of Jesus, I come boldly to Your throne of grace to receive mercy and find grace to help in time of need.

You have not given me a spirit of fear but a spirit of love, power, sound and personal discipline—abilities that result in a calm, well-balanced mind and self-control.

Forgive me for getting caught up in my own pride. Sometimes I behave as though I am indispensable at home, at the office, at church, and in other situations. I become irritable and fatigued, feeling that no one appreciates all that I do. Help me to step back and take a personal inventory. My spirit is Your candle, searching out all the inward parts of my being.

There is a time for everything, and a season for every activity under heaven. Help me to keep my priorities in order. Help me to fulfill my call and responsibilities at home. While I am at work, help me to stay focused. Also, help me to take time to find rest—relief, ease and refreshment and recreation and blessed quiet—for my soul.

I cast the whole of my care [all my anxieties, all my worries, all my concerns, once and for all] on You, for You care for me affectionately and care about me watchfully. I affirm that I am well-balanced (temperate, sober of mind), vigilant and cautious at all times.

To You be the dominion (power, authority, rule) for ever and ever. Amen (so be it).

SCRIPTURE
REFERENCES

Hebrews 4:16

2 Timothy 1:7 AMP

Ecclesiastes 3:1 NIV

Proverbs 20:27

Matthew 11:29 AMP

2 Corinthians 6:14

1 Peter 5:7-11 AMP

Committed to My Lord

FATHER, I pray that Your plan for my life will be fulfilled. My number one priority is to submit myself in love to You. I embrace Your truth rather than the basic principles of this world. I will not be conformed to the pattern of this world, but I ask to be transformed by the renewing of my mind. Then I will be able to test and approve what Your will is for me. I believe in Your Word, which is Your expressed will for my life.

Father, I purpose to obey You and remain in Your love. I love others and will show them by my actions. I commit and dedicate my whole body, mind, and spirit to You. I will serve You, my God, and keep Your commandments.

I will not follow the voice of a stranger. I choose my companions and friends carefully, according to Your Word, and determine to walk in paths of righteousness for Your name's sake.

Thank You that You chose me—actually picked me out for Yourself as Your own child—to be holy and blameless in Your sight.

I have made the decision to follow You as long as I live. I trust You to lead me and guide me through Your Word with the Holy Spirit as my Helper. I commit and trust my works to You — so that You cause my plans to be established and succeed. In Jesus' name I pray. Amen.

SCRIPTURE REFERENCES

Psalm 23:3 AMP

Psalms 37:4,5; 42:1

Proverbs 16:3 AMP

Jeremiah 29:13; 42:6

Lamentations 3:25

Luke 10:27

Acts 17:24,27,28

Romans 8:14,26; 12:2

1 Corinthians 15:33 AMP

Ephesians 1:4 AMP

Colossians 1:9; 2:20-22; 3:1-3

John 10:5 KJV; 14:16 AMP

Forgiven Always

FATHER, You did not send Jesus into the world to condemn me but that I might be saved. Thank You for the Holy Spirit, who is my constant Companion and Guide. Thank You for loving me and disciplining me as I'm renewing my mind to Your Word.

In agreement with Your Word, I choose to continue in the things which I have learned and been assured of, and I thank You for the Holy Scriptures that are able to make me wise for salvation through faith in Christ Jesus. Thank You for my Teacher who has taught me that all Scripture is profitable for doctrine, reproof, correction, and for instruction in righteousness that I am complete and thoroughly equipped for every good work.

Father, I repent and turn from my sin. I determine with Your help to make restitution when needed and make necessary changes in my life. Thank You for forgiving me and giving me a pure heart and renewing a right spirit within me. I am blessed because You have removed my transgressions from me as far as the east is from the west. You have removed the weight of sin and lifted the burden of guilt that has been weighing upon me. So by faith I receive my forgiveness, and thank You for cleansing me from all unrighteousness. In Jesus' name I pray. Amen.

SCRIPTURE REFERENCES

John 3:17

2 Timothy 3:15-16

Romans 6:13,14

Philippians 2:5,13

Proverbs 28:13

Romans 12:2

Hebrews 12:6-8

Psalm 103:2-4,8

Colossians 2:13,14 AMP

Acts 26:20

1 John 1:8-10

Always Forgiving

FATHER, in the name of Jesus I make a fresh commitment to You to live in peace—to get along with everybody—with my brothers and sisters in the body of Christ, with my friends, associates, neighbors, and family.

Father, I repent for holding onto bad feelings toward others. Today I let go of bitterness, rage, anger, harsh words and slander, and all other types of bad behavior. I ask You to forgive and release all who have wronged and hurt me. In the name of Jesus, I forgive and release them, and will show them kindness and mercy just as You have shown me.

From this moment on, I will be gentle and sensitive to others speaking kind words of encouragement to them. I will do what is right. I know that I have right-standing with You, Father, and You watch over Your children.

Thank You for Your love that has been poured into my heart by the Holy Spirit who is given to me. I believe that love touches everyone I know. Then all of us will be filled with the fruit of our salvation – which is the righteous character produced in our lives by Christ Jesus. So be it! Amen.

SCRIPTURE
REFERENCES

Romans 12:16-18 MSG

Romans 12:10

Philippians 2:2

Ephesians 4:31 NLT

Ephesians 4:27

Philippians 1:9,11 NLT

Mark 11:25

Ephesians 4:32 CEV

1 Peter 3:8,11,12 CEV

Colossians 1:10

Romans 5:5

Full of Praise and Thanksgiving

FATHER, I love You and praise You. I thank You for Your goodness and Your love. I'll continually thank You for Your mercy, which endures forever.

I praise You, Lord, and I will not forget all Your benefits. Thank You for forgiving my sins and for healing all my diseases. You fill my life with good things.

Father, You created the heavens, the earth, the sea, and everything in them. Thank You for making me so I can enjoy life to the fullest.

This is the day that You have made, and I rejoice and I am glad in it. You are my strength and my joy.

I thank You and praise You for supplying and providing everything I need. You are all-powerful, You know everything, and You are everywhere. Thank You for being such a loving Father to me that You gave Jesus to be my Savior, Lord, and Friend.

Thank You for sending the Holy Spirit to fill me, guide me, comfort me, and teach me the right things to do. I'll praise You in everything. In Jesus' name I pray. Amen.

SCRIPTURE
REFERENCES

Psalms 18:30; 24:1; 28:7;34:1; 48:1; 63:3,4,5; 71:8;
103:2,3,5,8; 106:1; 118:24; 136:1

Nehemiah 8:10

John 10:10 KJV; 14:16 AMP

Philippians 4:19   Revelation 4:8,11

PART II:

Looking to the Future

A Prayer for the Future

FATHER, I am dedicated to live for You. I don't know everything the future holds for me, but I know it is in Your hands. I trust You to lead me, to be my guide in life.

Thank You for preparing me now for Your life plan for me and for giving me the wisdom to discern the right timing for what You would have me do in each season of my life. I choose to love, obey, and cleave unto You with my whole body, soul, and spirit.

Help me to recognize the skills You have given me so I can develop them and give the glory to You. Give me understanding and light so I am quick to learn. I thank You for the wisdom and light that come from You and Your Word.

You are a help to me in everything I do. If it is Your will for me to marry someday, I thank You that You are not only preparing me, but You are also working on my future spouse. Until that time comes, help me to be content in every situation.

I believe that You will supply all the money I need to do Your will. I believe You will instruct me and teach me which way to go. You don't make things confusing for me, but You make a clear path for me when I put You first.

Thank You for Your words, which light my path, and for Your Holy Spirit, who reveals to me Your plan for me. I treasure my life with and for You. Thank You, Father, for holding my future and me in the palm of Your hand. In Jesus' name I pray. Amen.

SCRIPTURE REFERENCES

Deuteronomy 30:20	John 16:13
Psalms 25:5; 32:8; 119:105	Romans 8:14
1 Corinthians 2:9,10	Proverbs 3:5,6; 4:18
Ephesians 1:16-18; 2:10	Ecclesiastes 3:1-8
Philippians 4:11,13,19	Isaiah 49:16
Hebrews 13:5	Jeremiah 33:3

1 Peter 5:7

Decisions, Decisions

HEAVENLY Father, may I be filled with the clear knowledge of Your will in all wisdom and understanding. I know that Your will and Your Word agree. I will continue to meditate on Your Word so I can know Your plan and Your purpose for this season in my life. I want to live in a way that is worthy of You and fully pleasing to You. I believe You will cause my thoughts to agree with Your will so that I may be fruitful in every good work.

Your wisdom is pure and full of compassion. Teach me to love. I am growing strong in faith. Your words contain a wealth of wisdom.

As for this situation and decision today, I thank You for Your wisdom in knowing the right thing to do and to say. I listen to You. Teach me the way that You want me to go.

Thank You for counseling me and watching carefully over me. Thank You for the Holy Spirit. He is my Teacher, Helper, and Guide. I believe He is active in my life.

I won't be afraid or confused, because Your Word brings me light and understanding. Although there are many voices in the world, I will follow the voice of my Shepherd.

Thank You for wise counselors that You have put in my life to teach and instruct me. I will seek godly counsel from them. But when I need to make an important, final decision, I will follow the peace that comes from knowing Your Word.

I dedicate everything I do to You, knowing that my plans will succeed. I trust You with my life and everything in it. I thank You that to follow after You is to follow after peace in my heart. I thank You for Your wisdom. In Jesus' name I pray. Amen.

SCRIPTURE REFERENCES

Psalms 16:7; 32:8; 118:8; 119:99,130,133

John 10:15   1 Corinthians 14:33

Proverbs 2:6; 6:20-23; 19:21

Ephesians 5:15   Colossians 1:9; 3:16

Proverbs 16:3,9 AMP   James 1:5,6; 3:17

Joshua 1:9   1 John 5:14,15

Equipped for Success

THANK You, Father, that the teaching of Your Word gives light. The Word You speak (and I speak) is alive and full of power—making it active, operative, energizing, and effective. I receive the spirit of power and of love and of a calm and well-balanced mind and discipline and self-control that You have given to me. My qualification comes from You, and You have enabled me to be a minister of Your New Covenant—not of written laws but of the Spirit, who gives life.

In the name of Jesus, I submit to the destiny You planned for me before the foundation of the world. I give thanks to You, Father, for qualifying me to share in the inheritance of Your holy people in the kingdom of Light. Father, thank You for showing me that every "failure" is a learning experience and another stepping stone to success.

I belong to Christ, and I am a new person. The old life is gone, and a new life has begun. The past no longer controls my decisions. I forget the things that are behind and look forward to what lies ahead. I have been crucified with Christ, and I no longer live, but Christ lives in me. The life I now live in the body, I live by faith in the Son of God, who loved me and gave Himself for me.

Today I listen carefully to God's words. I don't lose sight of them. I let them penetrate deep into my heart, for they bring life to me and healing to my whole body. I guard my heart above all else, for it determines the course of my life.

Today I hold onto kindness and truth. I tie them around my neck and write them upon my heart so I will find favor and good understanding in the eyes of God and man.

Today my delight is in the teachings of the Lord and I reflect on them day and night. I am like a tree planted beside streams—a tree that produces fruit in season and whose leaves do not wither. I succeed in everything I do.

Thank You Father for the power Christ has given me. He leads me and makes me win in everything. Amen.

SCRIPTURE REFERENCES

Psalm 119:130 NLT

Hebrews 4:12 AMP

2 Timothy 1:7 AMP

2 Corinthians 3:5-6 NLT

Colossians 1:12-13 NIV

2 Corinthians 5:17 NLT

Philippians 3:13 NLT

Galatians 2:20 NIV

Proverbs 4:20-23 NLT

Proverbs 3:3-4 NLV

Letting Go of the Past

FATHER, I realize my helplessness in saving myself, and I honor and praise what Christ Jesus has done for me. I let go of the things I once considered valuable because I'm much better off knowing Jesus Christ my Lord. I throw it all away in order to gain Christ and to have a relationship with Him.

Lord, I have received Your Son, and He has given me the right to become Your child. I unfold my past and put into proper perspective those things that are behind. My old self has been crucified with Christ and I no longer live, but Christ lives in me. I live in this earthly body by faith in the Son of God who loved me and gave Himself for me. I trust in You, Lord, with all my heart and I do not depend on my own understanding. I seek to please You in all I do, and You show me which path to take.

I want to know Christ and experience the power that raised Him from the dead.

Whatever it takes, I will be one who lives in the fresh newness of life. I don't mean to say that I am perfect. I haven't learned all I should, but I keep working toward that day when I will finally be all that Christ saved me for and wants me to be.

I am bringing all my energies to bear on this one thing: Regardless of my past, I look forward to what lies ahead. I strain to reach the end of the race and receive the prize for which You are calling me up to heaven because of what Christ Jesus did for me. In Jesus' name I pray. Amen.

SCRIPTURE REFERENCES

Proverbs 3:5-6 NLT	John 1:12 NIV
Psalm 32:5 AMP	Romans 6:4 TLB
Philippians 3:13 NLT	Galatians 2:20 NIV
Philippians 3:12-14 TLB	Philippians 3:7-9 GW
Philippians 3:10-11 NLT	

Better Days Ahead

FATHER, I come asking You to hear my prayer. Listen, O God, and do not ignore my cry for help! Please listen and answer me, for I am overwhelmed by my troubles. I am scared, shaking, and terror has gripped me. I wish I had wings like a dove! Then I would fly away and rest. How quickly I would escape, far away from the wind and storm.

I call out to You God, and I know You will rescue me. You redeem my life in peace from this battle of hopelessness that has come against me. I pile my troubles on Your shoulders and thank You for carrying my load and helping me out. Hopelessness lies in wait to swallow me up or trample me all day long.

Whenever I am afraid, I choose to have confidence and put my trust and reliance in You. By Your help, God, I praise Your Word. On You I lean and put my trust. I do not entertain fear.

You keep track of all my sorrows. You have collected all my tears in Your bottle. You have recorded each one in Your book. Now I'm thanking You with all my heart. You pulled me from the brink of death, my feet from the cliff edge of doom. Now I stroll at leisure with You in the sunlit fields of life.

I am confident I will see Your goodness! I wait patiently for You, Lord. I am brave and courageous. Yes, I am waiting patiently.

Father, I give You all my worries and cares, for You care about me. I am well-balanced and cautious— alert, watching out for attacks from Satan, my great enemy. I am standing firm and strong in faith remembering that other Christians all around the world are going through the same kind of sufferings.

In the name of Jesus, I gain the victory by the blood of the Lamb and by the word of my witness. I look to the future, not the past. I look to better days ahead in Jesus' name. Amen.

SCRIPTURE REFERENCES

Hebrews 4:16 NIV

Psalm 55:1 MSG

Psalm 55:1-2 NLT

Psalm 55:5-8 NCV

Psalm 55:16 CEB

Psalm 55:18 AMP

Psalm 55:22 MSG

Psalm 56:8 NLT

Psalm 56:13 MSG

Psalm 27:13-14 NLT

1 Peter 5:7 NLT

1 Peter 5:8 AMP

1 Peter 5:8-9 NLT

Revelation 12:11 CEB

Psalm 56:2-4 AMP

Moving to a New Location

FATHER, Your Word says that You will work out Your plans for my life. Your faithful love endures forever. I bring to You my apprehensions concerning relocation. I ask that You go before me and my family to level the mountains in finding a new home.

Give me wisdom to make wise decisions in choosing the movers and packers best suited to handle our possessions. Cause me to find favor and earn a good reputation with You and people—with the utility companies, with the school systems, and with the banks—with everyone involved in this move.

Father, thank You for giving me new friends that You want me to have. I am trusting You to lead me to a church where I can worship together with other believers.

Lord, I depend on You for this move, knowing that You are my Provider. I enjoy serving You. I will seek to be a blessing to others.

I cast all these cares and concerns on You without fretting or worrying. I offer thanksgiving for this sense of God's wholeness, everything coming together for good will come and settle my mind. You are keeping me in perfect peace because my thoughts are fixed on You!

I trust in You, Lord, with all of my heart. I'm not depending on my own understanding. I will remember You in all I do and know that You will give me success.

Thank You, Father, for Your blessing on this move. In Jesus' name. Amen.

SCRIPTURE
REFERENCES

Psalm 138:8 NLT

Isaiah 45:2 NIV

James 1:5

Proverbs 3:4 NLT

Hebrews 10:25

Isaiah 26:3 NLT

Psalm 96:1

Psalm 98:1

Psalm 149:1

Psalm 37:4-5 NCV

Philippians 4:6,7 MSG

Proverbs 3:5,6

Trusting a Big God

ATHER, You are my God. I worship You with all my heart. I long for You just as I would long for a stream in a desert. I know that You hear me when I call to You for help. You are a big and powerful God, who rescues me from all my troubles.

It feels as though many things come against me, but You give me the victory! I depend on You and have chosen to trust You since I first believed. I can be sure that You will protect me from harm. In Christ, I have been made right with God, and my prayers have great power and produce wonderful results.

Jesus is the High Priest of my faith. I am completely free to enter the Most Holy Place without fear because of the blood of the Lamb. I can enter through a new and living way that Jesus opened for me. I am confident that You hear me whenever I ask for anything that pleases You. And since I know that you hear me when I make my requests, I also know that you will give me what I ask for.

In the moment that I get tired in the waiting, Holy Spirit, You are right alongside, helping me along. If I don't know how or what to pray, You help me pray, making prayer out of my wordless sighs and my aching groans. You know me far better than I know myself. This is why I can be so sure that every detail in my life is worked into something good.

In the name of Jesus, I will keep on being brave. I know it will bring me great rewards. I will learn to be patient so that I will please You, Lord, and receive what You have promised. I live by faith in the Son of God who loved me and gave Himself to save me. Hallelujah! Praise You Lord!

SCRIPTURE REFERENCES

Psalm 63:1 CEV

Psalm 34:17 NLT

Psalm 55:17 NCV

Psalm 71:5 CEV

Proverbs 3:26 CEV

Hebrews 10:35-36 CEV

Hebrews 3:1NCV

Hebrews 10:19-25NCV

1 John 5:14,15 NLT

Romans 8:26-28 MSG

1 Corinthians 1:30 NCV

James 5:16 NLT

Galatians 2:20 NIV

Direct My Steps

Lord, You are worthy to receive glory and honor and power. You created all things and by Your will they were created and have their being. You adopted me as Your child through Jesus Christ, in accordance with Your pleasure and will. As I share the faith I have in common with others, I pray that I may come to have a complete knowledge of all the good things I have in Christ.

Father, I ask You to fill me with a knowledge of Your will through all the wisdom and understanding that the Spirit gives so that I will live a life worthy of You, Lord, and please You in every way. Let my life bear fruit in every good work, as I grow in the knowledge of God.

I roll my works upon You, Lord, and You make my thoughts agreeable to Your will, so my plans are established and succeed. You direct and order my steps and make them sure. I will not act thoughtlessly but will learn what You want me to do. I pray that I will stand firm in all the will of God, mature, and fully assured.

Father, You have chosen me and make Your will known to me. Thank You, Holy Spirit, for leading me into all truth and telling me of things to come. God's Spirit and my spirit are in open communion. I am spiritually alive and have access to everything God's

Spirit is doing. Christ knows what God is doing, and I have His Spirit.

Father, I'm glad to have entered into Your rest and ceased from the weariness and pain of human labors. In Jesus' name I pray. Amen.

SCRIPTURE REFERENCES

Revelation 4:11NIV

Ephesians 1:5 NIV

Philemon 1:6 GW

Colossians 1:9-10 NIV

Proverbs 16:3,9 AMP

Colossians 4:12NIV

Acts 22:14WE

John 16:13 NLV

1 Corinthians 2:16 MSG

Hebrews 4:10 AMP

Ephesians 5:17 NCV

Pursuing God's Perfect Will

LORD and God, You are worthy to receive glory and honor and power, for You created all things; by Your will they were created. Thank You for adopting me as Your child through Jesus Christ, in accordance with Your pleasure and will. I pray that I may be active in sharing my faith, so that I will have a full understanding of every good thing I have in Christ.

Father, I ask You to give me a complete understanding of what You want to do in my life, and I ask You to make me wise with spiritual wisdom. Then the way I live will always honor and please You, and I will continually do good, kind things for others. All the while, I will learn to know You better and better.

Jesus has been made unto me wisdom. I single-mindedly walk in that wisdom, expecting to know what to do in every situation and to be on top of every circumstance.

I roll my works upon You [commit and trust them wholly to You: and You cause my thoughts to become agreeable to Your will, [and] so my plans are established and succeed. You direct my steps and make them sure. I understand and firmly grasp what Your will is, for I am not vague, thoughtless, and foolish. I stand firm and mature [in spiritual growth], convinced and fully assured in everything willed by You.

Father, You have destined and appointed me to come progressively to know Your will [to perceive, to recognize more strongly and clearly and to become better and more intimately acquainted with Your will].

I thank You, Father, for the Holy Spirit, who abides [permanently] in me and guides me into all truth (the whole, full truth) and speaks whatever He hears from You and announces and declares to me the things that are to come. I have the mind of Christ and do hold the thoughts (feelings and purposes) of His heart.

So, Father, I have entered into Your blessed rest by believing (trusting in, clinging to, and relying on) You. In Jesus' name I pray. Amen.

SCRIPTURE
REFERENCES

Philemon 6

Colossians 4:12 AMP

John 10:27

Acts 22:14 AMP

John 10:5

1 John 2:20,27 AMP

Colossians 1:9,10 AMP

John 16:13 AMP

1 Corinthians 1:30

1 Corinthians2:16 AMP

James 1:5-8

Hebrews 4:10 AMP

Proverbs 16:3,9 AMP

John 3:16 AMP

Ephesians 5:17 AMP

Proverbs 3:5,6

Psalm 119:105

John 14:26

Joshua 1:8

James 1:22

Great Is Your Faithfulness

FATHER, I ask for grace to trust You more. When I feel afraid I will trust in You. I praise Your Word. My God, in You I trust; I am not afraid. What can mortal man do to me?

Lord, Your steadfast love never ceases. Your mercies never come to an end.

They are new every morning, and great is Your faithfulness. You are my portion; therefore, I will hope in You.

May You, the God of hope, fill me with all joy and peace as I trust in You, so that I may overflow with hope by the power of the Holy Spirit.

To You, O Lord, I pray, and according to Your Word You will not fail me, for I am trusting You. None who has faith in You, Father, will ever be disgraced for trusting You.

Show me the path where I should go, O Lord. Point out the right road for me to walk. Lead me and teach me, for You are the God who gives me salvation.

Lord, I have no fear of bad news; my heart is steadfast, trusting in You. My heart is secure, and I will have no fear.

Because You are faithful and trustworthy, I make a commitment to trust in You with all my heart and lean not on my own understanding. In all my ways I acknowledge You, and You will make my paths straight. I am blessed, for I trust in the Lord, in whom is my confidence. In Jesus' name I pray. Amen.

SCRIPTURE REFERENCES

Psalm 56:3,4 NIV

Romans 15:13 NIV

Psalm 112:7,8 NIV

Jeremiah 17:7 NIV

Lamentations 3:22-24 RSV

Psalm 25:1-5 TLB

Proverbs 3:5,6 NIV

Light on the Path of Life

FATHER, I thank You that You are instructing me and teaching me in the way I should go and that You are guiding me with Your eye. I thank You for Your guidance and leadership concerning Your will, Your plan, and Your purpose for my life. I do hear the voice of the Good Shepherd, for I know You and follow You. You lead me in the paths of righteousness for Your name's sake.

In the name of Jesus, I refuse to be conformed to this world (this age), [fashioned after and adapted to its external, superficial customs], but I submit to the transformation by the [entire] renewal of my mind [by its new ideals and its new attitude], so that I may prove [for myself] what is Your good and acceptable and perfect will, even the thing which is good and acceptable and perfect [in Your sight for me].

Thank You, Father, that my path is growing brighter and brighter until it reaches the full light of day. As I follow You, Lord, I believe my path is becoming clearer each day.

Thank You, Father, that Jesus was made unto me wisdom. Confusion is not a part of my life. I am not confused about Your will for me. I trust in You and lean not unto my own understanding. As I acknowledge You in all my ways, You direct my paths.

I believe that as I trust in You completely, You will show me the path of life. Thank You, Father, in Jesus' name. Amen.

SCRIPTURE REFERENCES

Psalm 32:8	Proverbs 4:18
John 10:3,4	1 Corinthians 1:30
Psalm 23:3	Proverbs 3:5,6
Romans 12:2 AMP	Psalm 16:11

PART III:

Career & Workplace

Thankful for My Job

FATHER, thank You that You are my Provider and my Source of total supply. Every good thing that I have comes from You. Thank You that I am happy where I work, enjoying the results of my labor.

With Your help I will not grow tired of doing what is right but will develop a strong work ethic and have an excellent and enthusiastic attitude. Help me to be respectful to my employer. If something goes against my conscience, give me the words to communicate my objection in a clear and concise manner.

Help me to be an effective witness for the gospel by working hard, diligently, and quietly with a humble spirit at all times, not just when my boss is around. Help me to work as if I were working for You, because I am working for You.

Father, I am strong in You and the power of Your might. I will not give up but trust that my work will be recognized and rewarded. Thank You for Your protection so I don't have to be nervous or afraid of anything, but I share my requests with You in prayer. Thanks for Your peace that protects my heart and mind in every situation.

Father, please help me to have absolute and complete control over my tongue and what I say, so that I won't hurt or offend anyone. I won't murmur, complain, backbite, or gossip.

Thank You that I have favor with my boss and with all of the people I work with. In Jesus' name I pray. Amen.

SCRIPTURE REFERENCES

Deuteronomy 8:18

1 Chronicles 15:7

Proverbs 11:27 AMP

Ecclesiastes 5:18-20

Isaiah 48:17

John 6:43

Ephesians 6:5-7

Philippians 4:6,7,19

Colossians 3:23,24

1 Thessalonians 4:11,12

2 Thessalonians 3:13

James 1:5,17; 3:2

1 Corinthians 15:58

Wisdom in the Workplace

FATHER, I thank You for filling me with Your Spirit, giving me great wisdom, ability, and skill in accomplishing the work to which You have called me.

Thank You for imparting to me wisdom and understanding to know how to carry out all the affairs of my life and my job and its various tasks. My mouth shall speak of wisdom, and the meditation of my heart shall be of understanding.

I thank You that I am in Christ Jesus, who has become for me wisdom from You—that is, my righteousness, holiness, and redemption. I have become a reservoir of every kind of wisdom and spiritual understanding, and I choose to walk in the ways of true righteousness and please You in everything I do. I am a fruit-bearing branch that yields to You, maturing in the rich experience of knowing You in Your fullness and ever growing in You. In Jesus' name I pray. Amen.

SCRIPTURE
REFERENCES

Exodus 31:3 TLB   Colossians 1:9,10 NIV

1 Corinthians 1:30 NIV   Psalm 49:3

Exodus 36:1

Commitment to My Employer

D EAR Father, as an employee, I consider myself a team member yoked together with my employer and co-workers. So, gladly I assume my share of the workload and set my heart to serve others. I consider my employer worthy of full respect, so that God's name and His teachings may not be slandered. It will never be said that I am a poor worker.

I agree to the sound instruction of my Lord Jesus Christ and to godly teaching. I refuse to quibble over the meaning of Christ's words and to stir up arguments ending in jealousy and anger, which only lead to name-calling, accusations, and evil suspicions. I will tell the truth at all times.

Godliness with contentment is great gain. For I brought nothing into the world, and I can take nothing out of it. I have food and clothing, and I am content with that.

I understand that the love of money is a root of all kinds of evil and causes all kinds of trouble, so that some people want money so much that they have given up their faith and caused themselves a lot of pain. My motive for working is not to get rich. I would not wander from the faith and pierce myself with many griefs. Instead, I work that I may have something to share with those in need.

I set aside hidden agendas and factional motives. In the true spirit of humility, I am not jealous or proud but humble, and I consider others more important than myself. I care and esteem my employer and co-workers as much as I care and esteem myself. I am concerned for their interests as well as my own. I will not allow self-promotion to hide in my heart. I have the mind of Christ and His mindset is my motivation. He is my example in humility and all things.

Thank You, Father, for creating in me a servant's heart and attitude. In Jesus' name I pray. Amen.

SCRIPTURE REFERENCES

1 Timothy 6:1-10 NIV   Ephesians 4:28 NIV

1 Timothy 6:1-10 TLB   Philippians 2:3-5 AMP

Daily Dedication

FATHER, I thank You and praise You for this day. I dedicate myself, afresh and anew, to You and to Your service. I commit to live and operate today according to Your Word and the principles and precepts that You have established in it.

I place myself in Your hands. I submit my will to Your will. In Your Word, You have promised that You will give me wisdom in the affairs of life. I receive Your wisdom in every decision I make. Help me to consider both sides of every issue, to see all the facts involved in every situation and to think clearly and accurately.

When I encounter situations or become involved in circumstances beyond my knowledge or experience, I will yield to the Holy Spirit, whom You have sent to reveal to me all things. I will ask Him to minister to me, lead me, guide me, and direct me in the truth concerning every matter I have to deal with today.

I choose by an act of my will to be the very best employee that I can be this day, to give my employer 100 percent of my time, my effort, and my loyalty.

Father, according to Your Word, everything that I set my hand to shall prosper. I thank You, Lord, that my work shall prosper today. Show me mistakes before they occur and reveal to me how to be more effective and efficient in my work. Help me to bring glory and honor to You in every action I take, every deed I perform, and every word I speak.

Thank You that my mind is active and alert. I put out of my thoughts all my personal concerns, and I focus totally on the work before me, giving full attention to the duties and responsibilities that have been assigned me this day.

I thank You that my enthusiasm for my job will be evident to all concerned, and that the excellent way I perform my duties will be a witness to everyone who comes in contact with me.

I choose to be patient and kind to all those who work with me. Thank You that the faithful shall abound in blessings. No matter what the situation, regardless of the circumstances, I will respond in love and in truth. I will not seek my own way or try to promote myself, but I will be secure in the knowledge that if I am faithful and diligent to do my job to the best of my ability, then recognition and promotion will come—from You.

I refuse to lift up myself, to try to force myself into a position of prominence so that others will notice me. I simply commit myself to do whatever I have been assigned to do with all my strength and might and heart and soul.

Thank You that my honest efforts and godly attitude will become obvious to my superiors so that pay increases and promotions will follow as a matter of course. Help me always to be on the lookout for ways to increase my contribution to the success of my department and the company as a whole. In this way, I will find favor with You and with others. In Jesus' name I pray. Amen.

SCRIPTURE REFERENCES

Psalm 118:24

Romans 12:2

Proverbs 4:20-22 AMP

2 Timothy 2:24 NIV

James 4:7

Proverbs 10:22

Proverbs 2:7

Psalm 75:6,7

John 16:13

Ephesians 6:10

Deuteronomy 28:12

Psalm 5:12

1 Corinthians 2:16

Prayer for the Company

FATHER, I pray for my place of employment today. I thank You for this organization and for the opportunity to be a part of it. I am grateful for the chance to earn the income this firm provides for me and for the blessing it has been to me and all its employees.

Father, I thank You that the company enjoys a good reputation, that it is seen well in the minds of its customers and vendors. Thank You that it prospers and makes a profit, that You give it favor with its clients, that You continue to provide wisdom and insight to those within it who occupy important decision-making positions.

It is my prayer that it will continue to thrive and prosper. Thank You for increased sales and expanded markets. Thank You, Father, for the creativity that is evident in the different areas of the company—new product ideas, new servicing concepts, new innovations and techniques—that keep this organization vibrant, alive, and thriving.

I ask You, Lord, to bless it and to cause it to be a blessing to the market it serves, as well as to all those whose lives are invested in it on a daily basis. In Jesus' name I pray. Amen.

SCRIPTURE REFERENCES

1 Timothy 2:1-3

3 John 2

Joshua 1:8

Psalm 5:12

Proverbs 2:7

Proverbs 3:21

Psalm 115:14

Proverbs 8:12

Malachi 3:12 AMP

Hebrews 6:14

Prayer for My Employers

FATHER, in the name of Jesus, I thank You for the privilege of serving You as an employee here at _____. I ask You to send Your Holy Spirit to teach me to pray for the good of the company, that Your name may be glorified. I pray for those who are in positions of authority and leadership in it. I offer this prayer on behalf of the company executives, asking that You turn their hearts in the way that You would have them go.

I pray for the president and other officers, thanking You for their commitment and dedication to this organization. Thank You that they are upright and honest in all their business dealings. Thank You for providing them new and creative ideas on how to better fulfill their duties and responsibilities and complete the tasks that You have entrusted to them.

Give them insight and understanding beyond their reason. Thank You for Your anointing upon them that goes far beyond their natural gifts and talents. Give them, I pray, clear and distinct direction so they know what to do and how to do it. Grant them the vision to develop new ideas and concepts and the ability to implement them for the good of all concerned.

Help them, Father, to be sensitive to the needs of every individual in this company. Give them the ability to balance the financial and human resources available to them. Give them supernatural foresight and discernment concerning personnel matters.

Thank You, Father, that they receive all the pertinent information necessary to make good and correct decisions. Help me to be a blessing to them, to respect them, and to give honor where honor is due. May I always be an asset to them and never a liability.

Thank You that when we pray in obedience to Your will for those who occupy positions of authority or high responsibility, outwardly, we will experience a quiet and undisturbed life and, inwardly, a peaceable one in all godliness and reverence and seriousness in every way.

During these days of constant change, help those in authority to maintain a positive attitude and to count it all joy when they fall into various trails, knowing that the testing of their faith produces patience. Help them to remember that patience is a force that will enable them to persevere.

In the name of Jesus, I command the spirit of fear to be far from the owners and directors of this organization. Clothed in the armor of God, I stand against any pressure and anxiety that would cause them to make hasty or unwise decisions. Help them to discern between good and bad choices and to make wise decisions—decisions that will contribute to the growth of this company and work for the benefit of every employee. In Jesus' name I pray. Amen.

SCRIPTURE REFERENCES

2 Thessalonians 1:12

Proverbs 21:1

Psalm 25:21

Romans 12:17 NIV

Ephesians 1:9,17

Proverbs 3:5,6

1 Timothy 2:1-3

Isaiah 33:6

James 1:2-4

Hebrews 10:35,36

2 Timothy 1:7

Ephesians 6:11-18

Psalm 37:23 AMP

Prayer for a Superior

FATHER, in Your Word, You said to pray for those who exercise authority over us, so I pray for my manager/supervisor today. I ask You to give him/her clarity of thought concerning each decision made this day. Help him/her to clearly identify and accurately assess every potential problem. Help him/her to make the right decisions—to respond, and not to react to whatever situation or circumstance might arise during the course of the day.

I ask You, Father, to help him/her to set the proper priorities today. Reveal to him/her what tasks are most important and cause him/her to inspire us to perform our duties to the best of our abilities.

I ask that You help him/her to be sensitive to the needs of those under his/her supervision, those who work for him/her. Help him/her to realize that not everyone is the same and that no two people respond or react in the same way. Help him/her to adapt his/her management style or technique to the strengths, weaknesses, and personality type of each individual. Grant him/her the ability to manage beyond his/her own natural gifts and talents. I pray that he/she will rely upon You, drawing strength, wisdom, and insight from You.

I purpose in my heart to set a guard over my mouth. I refuse to say anything negative or disrespectful about my manager/supervisor. I choose to support him/her and to say only good things about him/her.

Lord, I ask You to give him/her a peaceful spirit, so that even in the midst of great turmoil he/she may act with surety and confidence and make wise decisions. Help me to be sensitive to his/her needs and responsibilities. Show me ways, Lord, to support him/her and to assist him/her in the performance of his/her duties.

Father, You have said in Your Word that Your Spirit will show us things to come. I ask You to show my manager/supervisor the solution to small problems before they become major problems. Grant him/her creative ideas on how he/she can better lead and manage his/her department.

For all these things I give You thanks, praise, and glory in Jesus' name. Amen.

SCRIPTURE REFERENCES

1 Timothy 2:1-3 AMP

1Corinthians 2:16

Ephesians 4:23,24

Matthew 6:33 AMP

Romans 12:10

Isaiah 40:29-31 AMP

Philippians 4:7

Hebrews 12:14

John 14:26

John 16:13

Giving 100%

LORD, help me today to do my very best. I give myself 100 percent to my company.

Help me to be the most valuable worker possible, one who is sensitive to the needs of his co-workers and responsive to the desires of his employer. I purpose to perform my duties with a spirit of excellence, to do all that is required of me, and even above and beyond that which is required of me, that I may be a blessing to others and an asset to this company.

Lord, I purpose in my heart to fulfill my duties to the best of my ability. I vow never to shirk my responsibilities or to be slack in my work. If I make a mistake, I will be open and honest and forthright, admitting it and doing all I can to correct it.

I make a commitment not to try to impress anybody but to do my job humbly, quietly, effectively, and efficiently. I will not stretch the truth or give the impression that something is true when it's not. I will not be lax or lazy but will be conscientious and trustworthy in all my business dealings.

I will do my best to establish and maintain good relationships with my co-workers and superiors. I am committed to be a faithful, devoted worker. Whatever my hand touches, that I will do with all my might, with all my energy, with all that is within me.

I will do everything in my power to become the most productive employee in this organization. I solemnly pledge that I will be nothing but a blessing to it.

I know, Lord, that promotion comes from You. I thank You that the faithful will be rewarded and that I will abound in blessings. Thank You that my attitude, commitment, and performance on the job will become obvious to those for whom I work and that recognition, promotion, benefits, and raises will follow as a matter of course.

Thank You for the opportunity to see You show Yourself strong on my behalf. I call upon the Greater One who is in me today to provide me strength, knowledge, wisdom, and ability beyond my human limits. Thank You that I operate supernaturally today, by the power of Your indwelling Spirit so that I am able to perform my duties with outstanding accuracy and excellence. In Jesus' name I pray. Amen.

SCRIPTURE REFERENCES

Proverbs 16:3 NIV

Daniel 5:12 AMP

Proverbs 17:27 AMP

Proverbs 10:4

Proverbs 22:29 NIV

Colossians 3:17

Proverbs 28:20

2 Chronicles 16:9

1 John 4:4

Psalm 75:6,7

Romans 12:17 NIV

Persecution at Work

FATHER, I come to You in the name that is above all other names—the name of Jesus. Your name is a strong tower that I can run into and be safe when I am persecuted on the job.

Lord, I admit that these unkind words really hurt me. I desire to be accepted by my boss and co-workers, but I long to obey You and follow Your commandments. I know that Jesus was tempted just as I am, but He didn't give in to sin or hate. Please give me Your mercy and grace to deal with this situation. I look to You for my comfort. You are a true Friend at all times.

Thank You, Lord, for never leaving me alone or rejecting me. I make a decision to forgive the people who have spoken unkind words about me. I ask You to work this forgiveness in my heart. I submit to You and reject the disappointment and anger that have attempted to consume me. Specifically, right now I forgive

_____ .

I ask You to cause this situation to accommodate itself for good in my life. I offer You my heart, Lord, and I trust You. Don't allow my foes to gloat over me or the shame of defeat to overtake me. I have entwined my heart with You, and therefore, my enemies cannot triumph over me. I will call upon You, and You will deliver me. You will be with me in trouble. You will deliver me and honor me.

Because I love You, O Lord, You will rescue me. You will protect me because I acknowledge Your name. I will call upon You, and You will deliver me. You will be with me in trouble. You will deliver me and honor me.

Father, I will resist the temptation to strike back in anger. I purpose to love with the love of Jesus in me. Mercy and truth are written upon the tablets of my heart; therefore, You will cause me to find favor and understanding with my boss and co-workers. Keep me from self-righteousness so that I may walk in Your righteousness. Thank You for sending and giving me friends who will stand by me and teach me how to guard my heart with all diligence.

I declare that in the midst of all these things I am more than a conqueror through Jesus, who loves me. I can use the witty inventions You have provided me, and I will be confident in Your wisdom when working. I am of good courage and pray that freedom of utterance be given to me as I do my job. In Jesus' name I pray. Amen.

SCRIPTURE REFERENCES

Philippians 2:9

Proverbs 18:10

Hebrews 4:15

Proverbs 17:17

Hebrews 13:5

Proverbs 16:4 AMP

Psalm 91:14,15 NIV

Proverbs 3:3,4

Proverbs 4:23

Romans 8:37

Proverbs 8:12

Psalm 31:24

Ephesians 6:19

Psalm 25:1,2

Passed Over for Promotion

FATHER, in the name of Jesus, I come before Your throne of grace with confidence to receive mercy and find grace in my time of need. I feel that my employer has been unfair to me in the recent changes within the company. Another person has been promoted to the position for which I aspire and even now believe I rightfully deserve.

I cannot change this situation, so I look to You to help me overcome anger and disappointment. Forgive me for the accusations I have made against my boss. I come to You in repentance, capturing my thoughts and making them obey Jesus Christ.

Lord, it is You who pours out more and more grace upon us, for Your Word says You resist us when we're proud but continually pour out grace when we're humble. I choose to live well, live wisely, and live humbly. I choose wisdom that comes from above that leads me to be pure, friendly, gentle, sensible, kind, helpful, genuine, and sincere. I am a peacemaker who plants seeds of peace and harvests justice.

Your Word says to rejoice with those who rejoice, so I rejoice with the person who has been promoted. I realize, Lord, that this individual would not have received this promotion if he/she had not deserved it.

I put my own feelings aside and pray for Your richest blessing upon him/her. I refuse to allow a root of bitterness toward this person or the company to spring up in my heart and poison my life. I refuse to hold anyone accountable for this situation but entrust it entirely to You.

Lord, I place my situation, my future, into Your hand, committing with greater assurance than ever to do my very best with the gifts and talents You have given me. If there are any bad habits in my work or improper attitudes in my heart that would keep me from being promoted, I ask You to reveal them to me and help me to overcome them.

I will not seek to promote myself or to bring myself to the attention of people, but I will bring myself to Your attention by doing my job to the best of my ability.

Help me to write love and faithfulness upon the tablets of my heart. Then I will win favor and a good name in the sight of God and man. I choose to trust in You with all my heart and lean not on my own understanding. In all my ways, I acknowledge You, and You will make my paths straight.

I refuse the pressure to make a hasty decision, remembering that careful planning puts me ahead in the long run; hurry and scurry puts me further behind.

I humble myself, therefore, under the mighty hand of God so that at the proper time He may exalt me, casting all my anxieties on Him, because He cares for me.

Father, I look to You for well-timed promotions. For not from the east, nor from the west, nor from the south come promotion and lifting up but from You, Lord, the righteous Judge. In Jesus' name I pray. Amen.

SCRIPTURE REFERENCES

Hebrews 4:16 AMP	Hebrews 12:15
1 Corinthians 10:5	Proverbs 3:3-6 NIV
James 4:6 AMP	Proverbs 21:5 NIV
James 3:13 AMP	James 4:10 AMP
Romans 12:15	Psalm 75:6

Priorities

FATHER, too often I waste my time on useless, mere busy-work, and I am asking You to help me establish the correct priorities in my work. I confess my weakness of procrastination and lack of organization. I want to use my head and make the most of every chance I get!

You have given me a seven-day week—six days to work and the seventh day to rest. I want to make the most of every day You have given me. Help me to plan my time and stay focused on my assignments.

In the name of Jesus, I break down every big idea, thought, or imagination that tries to stop me from following you. I take every thought prisoner to make it obey You, Lord. I lay aside weight and distraction because I want to live a life of obedience to You.

Lord, You are the One who makes my plans succeed. I plan my way, but You direct my steps and make them sure. I trust You to help me organize my efforts, schedule my activities, and budget my time.

Jesus, You want me to relax, and You will show me how to take a real rest and learn the unforced rhythms of grace. If I keep company with You, I will learn to live freely and lightly.

By the grace given to me, I will not worry about missing out, and my everyday human concerns will be met. I will work first for

Your kingdom, do what You call good, and then I will have all the other things I need.

Father, You sent Jesus that I might live and enjoy life to the full. So I give all my worries and cares to You because You care about me. I cry out for insight and raise my voice for understanding. I make insight my priority! In Jesus' name. Amen.

SCRIPTURE REFERENCES

Ephesians 5:15-16 MSG	Genesis 2:2 NIV
2 Corinthians 10:5-6 WE	Proverbs 16:3,9 AMP
Matthew 11:29 MSG	Colossians 2:10 NCV
Matthew 6:33 WE	1 Peter 5:7-8 NLT
Proverbs 2:3 AMP	John 10:10 WE

Using Discretion

FATHER, I thank You for the virtue of discretion. You give me knowledge and discretion. Discretion protects me and understanding guards me.

I preserve sound judgment and discernment. I will not let them out of my sight. I wear their teachings as you would a lovely hat or a pretty necklace. Then I will go on my way in safety, and not stumble. When I lie down, I will not be afraid. When I lie down, my sleep will be sweet. I have no fear of sudden disaster or of the ruin that overtakes the wicked, for You, Lord, will be my confidence, my help, my protection.

Father, I pay attention to Your wisdom and sound judgment. I always keep them in mind. Godly discretion defers anger and gives me patience; it enables me to overlook an offense.

Father, You are my God and my Teacher; You instruct me in discretion.

All this comes from You, the Lord Almighty. You are wonderful in counsel and magnificent in wisdom. Praise the Lord! In Jesus' name I pray. Amen.

SCRIPTURE
REFERENCES

Proverbs 1:4

Proverbs 2:11 NIV

Proverbs 3:21-26 NIV

Proverbs 5:1,2 NIV

Proverbs 19:11

Proverbs 19:11 NIV

Isaiah 28:26

Isaiah 28:29 NIV

Displaying Integrity

FATHER, when You test my heart, may You be pleased with my honesty. In everything I do, may I set an example by doing what is good.

In my place of business, may I show integrity, seriousness, and soundness of speech that cannot be condemned, so that those who oppose me may be ashamed because they have nothing bad to say about me. I purpose to manage, as David did, with integrity of heart; with skillful hands he led the people.

Father, I thank You that the integrity of the upright guides me. May I be blameless in Your sight so that I will receive a good inheritance. Let it be said of me by all individuals, "We know you are a person of integrity. You treat everyone with the same respect, no matter who they are."

Judge me, Lord, according to my righteousness and integrity. Show that I am honest and innocent. You know every heart and mind, and You always do right. You, dear Father, are my shield, the protector of everyone whose heart is right. In my integrity, You uphold me and will always be close to my side. In Jesus' name I pray. Amen.

SCRIPTURE REFERENCES

1 Chronicles 29:17 NIV

Titus 2:7,8 NIV

Psalm 78:12 NIV

Proverbs 11:3 NIV

Matthew 22:16 NIV

Psalm 7:8 NIV

Proverbs 13:5 NIV

Psalm 41:12 NIV

Proverbs 28:10 NIV

Dealing with Strife

FATHER, I come to You in the name above all other names—the name of Jesus. Your name is a strong tower that I can run into and be safe when I encounter strife on the job.

Lord, I admit that the accusations and unkind words spoken to me and about me really hurt. I desire to be accepted by my employer/co-workers/employees, but I long to obey You and follow Your commandments. I know that Jesus was tempted just as I am, but He didn't give in to sin or hate. Please give me Your mercy and grace to deal with this situation. I look to You for my comfort; You are a true Friend at all times.

Thank You, Lord, for never leaving me alone or rejecting me. I make a decision to forgive the people who have spoken unkind words about me. I ask You to work this forgiveness in my heart. I submit to You and reject the disappointment and anger that have attempted to consume me.

Specifically, right now I forgive _____ .

I ask You to cause this situation to accommodate itself for good in my life and in the lives of others. You have said, "If you love Me and truly know who I am, I will rescue you and keep you safe." Thank You, Lord, that I will not be put to shame, nor will my enemies triumph over me. I will call upon You, and You will deliver me. You will be with me in trouble, and You will deliver me and honor me.

Father, I will resist the temptation to strike back in anger. I purpose to love with the love of Jesus in me. Mercy and truth are written upon the tablets of my heart; therefore, You will cause me to find favor and understanding with my employer, co-workers, and employees. Keep me from self-righteousness so that I may walk in Your righteousness.

Thank You for giving me friends who will stand by me and teach me how to guard my heart with all diligence.

I declare that through all these things I am more than a conqueror through Jesus, who loves me. I will be confident in Your wisdom as I continue to do my job. In Jesus' name I pray. Amen.

SCRIPTURE REFERENCES

Philippians 2:9

Psalm 25:1,2 NIV

Proverbs 4:23

Romans 8:37

Proverbs 8:12

Psalm 31:24

Ephesians 6:19

Proverbs 3:3,4

Proverbs 18:10

Hebrews 4:15

Proverbs 17:17

Hebrews 13:5

Proverbs 16:4 AMP

Psalm 91:14,15 NIV

Overcoming Negative Work Attitudes

FATHER, You see the struggle I am having with my employers and fellow employees. I desire to put off the negative attitudes and put on positive attitudes. I bind mercy, love, discernment and kindness to my mind, and loose all judgments and bad feelings toward others from my mind. I ask You, Holy Spirit, to remind me of godly instruction. My heart will store the commands of my Father. Your words that I've hidden in my heart will enable me to live a long time and provide me with well-being. Thank You for creating in me loyalty and faithfulness. I tie them on my neck and write them deep within my heart. Then I will find favor and approval in Your eyes and in the eyes of my employers and fellow employees.

God, You are the One who enables me both to want and to actually live out Your good purposes at my place of employment. I do everything without grumbling and arguing so that I may be blameless and pure, Your innocent child.

I hear Your Word and do Your Word, not working to make myself look good or flattering people at my workplace, but I act like a slave of Christ, carrying out Your will from my heart. I serve my employer enthusiastically, as though I am serving You,

Lord, and I know that You will reward every person who does what is right.

I honor You, my Lord, and my work is a sincere expression of my devotion to You. In the name of Jesus. Amen.

SCRIPTURE REFERENCES

Proverbs 3:1-4 CEB   Jeremiah 1:12 MSG

Colossians 3:22-24 NLT   Ephesians 6:5-8CEB

Philippians 2:14,15 NCV

Manifesting Gentleness

FATHER, I desire to be a leader controlled by Your wisdom, which is full of quiet gentleness. Reveal to me by Your Spirit how to be equitable, fair, moderate, and forbearing in dealing with my co-workers. I desire to look at situations humanely and reasonably rather than insisting on the letter of the law.

In the name of Jesus, I will not be combative but gentle and kind and considerate, not quarrelsome but forbearing and peaceable, and not a lover of money. I seek to be submissive, obedient, prepared, and willing to do any upright and honorable work.

I will not slander or abuse or speak evil of anyone (my co-workers, customers, friends, family members, or competitors). I avoid contentiousness. In the name of Jesus, I am forbearing (yielding, gentle, and conciliatory), and I will show unqualified courtesy and gentleness toward everybody. True love for God means obeying His commandments, which never weigh us down as heavy burdens.

I recognize that gentleness is love in action—being considerate, meeting the needs of others, allowing time for the other person to talk and being willing to listen and learn. Help me maintain a gentle attitude in my relationships with others. In Jesus' name I pray. Amen.

SCRIPTURE
REFERENCES

James 3:17 TLB   1 Timothy 3:3

Titus 3:1-3 AMP   1 Thessalonians 2:7 NIV

Showing Mercy

FATHER, in the name of Jesus, I am Your child and an imitator of You. You are so rich in mercy that You gave me back my life even though I was spiritually dead and doomed by my sins. It was by Your undeserved favor toward me that I was redeemed and set free. At Your invitation, I pray boldly for mercy for myself and for my associates, competitors, family, and friends.

As Your chosen child, holy and dearly loved, I clothe myself with compassion, kindness, humility, gentleness, and patience. I bear with others and forgive whatever grievances I may have against them. I forgive as You, Lord, forgave me. And over all these virtues I put on love, which binds them all together in perfect unity.

Help me to make allowances for another's faults, realizing that through gentleness and humility I might help him back onto the right path, while remembering that the next time I may be the one in the wrong.

Help me and my co-workers to share each other's trouble and problems appropriately. Let us be sure that we are doing our very best, for then we will have the personal satisfaction of work well done and won't need to compare ourselves with someone else. Each of us must bear some faults and burdens of his own, for none of us is perfect.

Father, I renounce self-righteousness and pride that would cause me to despise others and cut me off from Your mercy. Jesus said that if I am merciful to others, I will be shown mercy. Therefore, I choose to manifest mercy. In Jesus' name I pray. Amen.

SCRIPTURE REFERENCES

Ephesians 5:1 NIV

Galatians 6:1-5 TLB

Colossians 3:12-14 NIV

Hebrews 4:16

Ephesians 2:4 TLB

Matthew 5:7 NIV

Prayer Before Travel

FATHER, today, in Jesus' name, I speak Your words over my travel plans knowing that Your words do not return empty, but they make things happen that You want to happen. They succeed in doing what You send them to do. Thank You for watching to make sure Your words come true.

As I prepare to travel, I remember it is You alone, Lord, who keeps me safe. I live under the protection of God Most High. If I face any problems or trouble, You are a mighty tower that I can run to for safety. My trust is in the Lord and I am safe. Believing in the written Word of God, I speak peace, safety, and success over my travel plans.

As Your child, my path of travel is guarded by You, and my life is protected. You order Your angels to protect me wherever I go. I will proceed with my travel plans without fear of accidents, problems, or any type of frustrations. You have given me a calm, well-balanced mind. I have Your peace and it guards my heart and mind as I live in Christ Jesus. Thank You, Father, that in every situation, You are there to protect me. No matter what means of transportation I choose for travel, You will protect me. You are my heavenly Father, and I belong to You. Through my faith in You, I have the power to trample on snakes and scorpions and to overcome all the power of the enemy—nothing will harm me. Even if I were to contact something poisonous, it will not hurt me. In fact, I'm able to place my hands on the sick, and they will be healed.

Whatever I forbid on earth will be forbidden in heaven and whatever I permit on earth will be permitted in heaven. I can ask for anything in the name of Jesus and He will do it, so that the Son can bring glory to the Father. (Asking in the name of Jesus indicates I am asking in agreement with His will.)

Father, I honor You and Your mercy is upon me and my family, and our travels will be safe. Thank You for Your guidance and safety—You are worthy of all praise. Amen.

SCRIPTURE REFERENCES

Isaiah 55:11NCV

Jeremiah 1:12 NCV

Psalm 4:8 NLT

Psalm 91:1 CEV

Proverbs 18:10 CEV

Proverbs 29:25 GW

Mark 11:23-24 NIV

Proverbs 2:8 NLT

Psalm 91:11-12 NLT

2 Timothy 1:7 AMP

2 Timothy 4:18 NIV

Isaiah 43:1-3 NCV

Luke 10:19 NIV

Psalm 91:13 CEV

Mark 16:18 NLT

Matthew 18:18NLT

John 14:13 NLT

Daniel 9:18 NIV

Luke 1:50 GNT

Luke 21:18 NIV

Philippians 4:7 NLT

Prayer at Quitting Time

FATHER, I thank You for this day, but I do not carry the baggage of the day home with me. I leave it at work. Whatever responsibilities, problems, or situations I had to face there, however difficult the day may have been for me, I give it all to You. By an act of my will, I choose not to think about it, meditate on it, or allow it to control my life.

With the same zeal, enthusiasm, and fervor that I started this day, I now turn toward my home life, family, and friends. I refuse to drag across the threshold of my home weary, worn out, and beaten down by the day's activities.

Father, grant me a refreshing now for the second part of my day. Thank You that Your joy overflows in my heart so that I come home as a solution, not a problem. As I enter the doorway, let me bring with me joy, peace, and life, not misery, frustration, and fatigue.

Lord, I ask You to strengthen me: spirit, soul, and body. Fill my heart with Your love and grace. Clear my mind of the cobwebs of the day. Thank You that I can choose to put a smile on my face and joy in my heart, that I can determine in advance to have a wonderful evening.

Help me never to speak ill about anyone in my workplace or say anything that will give my family and friends wrong thoughts or ideas or attitudes toward my work.

Thank You for the gift of Your Holy Spirit to empower me for the work You have called me to do and to know when it is time to leave it behind. In Jesus' name I pray. Amen.

SCRIPTURE REFERENCES

Psalm 19:14

Psalm 28:7

Proverbs 17:22

Isaiah 40:29 NIV

Isaiah 41:10 AMP

Psalm 127:3-5

Joel 3:10

Ephesians 4:32

1 Timothy 4:14

Proverbs 15:23 AMP

Romans 13:10 AMP

Acts 1:8

PART IV:

$$$ Wisdom

God is My Source

ATHER, thank You for being my Source of everything good. Before I even ask, You know my financial needs. You said that the things I desire (in accordance with Your will) will be given to me if I ask You. Because I trust You, I ask specifically for $ _____ to meet my present financial need.

Thank You for my job and salary. I'm am grateful for it, and I bless my employer.

But I recognize You as my Source. I won't worry, because I have You to provide for my every financial need. Your Word says that You take pleasure in the prosperity of Your servant.

Because You have given me the ability to obtain wealth, I will look for good ideas and opportunities to earn the money that I need. I will keep a good attitude and work hard. Thank You for giving me favor with others.

Your Word promises that since I have given my tithes and offerings to You cheerfully, without complaining, I will always have enough. I will stay faithful and thankful to You and to people You use to meet my needs. Because I am Your child, I believe You will bless those who bless me.

Please help me to learn to handle my money wisely. Thank You for meeting my financial needs so that I can prosper and enjoy life to the fullest. In Jesus' name I pray. Amen.

SCRIPTURE REFERENCES

Genesis 12:2,3	Isaiah 65:24
Numbers 23:19	Malachi 3:10,11
Deuteronomy 8:18; 28:1-13	Matthew 6:32,33
Luke 6:38	Psalms 23:1; 34:10
Proverbs 3:4,9,10; 10:4	James 1:17
Ecclesiastes 5:19	1John 5:14,15

Prosperity

FATHER, I come to You, in the name of Jesus, concerning my financial situation. You are a very present help in trouble, and You are more than enough. Your Word declares that You shall supply all my need according to Your riches in glory by Christ Jesus.

(If you have not been giving tithes and offerings, include this statement of repentance in your prayer.) Father, forgive me for robbing You in tithes and offerings. I repent and purpose to bring all my tithes into the storehouse, that there may be food in Your house. Thank You for wise financial counselors and teachers who are teaching me the principles of good stewardship.

Lord of hosts, You said, "Try Me now in this, and I will open the windows of heaven and pour out for you such blessing that there will not be room enough to receive it." You will rebuke the devourer for my sake. My heart is filled with thanksgiving.

Lord, my God, I shall remember that it is You who give me the power to get wealth, that You may establish Your covenant. In the name of Jesus, I worship You only, and I will have no other gods before me.

You are able to make all grace—every favor and earthly bless-ing—come to me in abundance, so that I am always, and in all circumstances, furnished in abundance for every good work and charitable donation. Amen.

SCRIPTURE REFERENCES

Psalm 56:1

Philippians 4:19

Deuteronomy 8:18-19

2 Corinthians 9:8 AMP

Malachi 3:8-12

Tithing

THANK you, Father, that I have come into the inheritance which You gave me in Christ Jesus. Your mercy is great, and You love me very much. Though I was spiritually dead, when I acknowledged Jesus as my Lord, You gave me new life with Christ. I have been saved by Your grace. You rescued me from the kingdom of darkness and transferred me into the kingdom of Your dear Son.

Jesus, as my Lord and High Priest, I bring the first portion of my income to You and worship the Lord my God with it.

Father, I celebrate because of all the good things You have given to me. I have obeyed You and done everything You commanded me. Now look down from Your holy dwelling place in heaven and bless me as You said in Your Word. Thank You, Father, in Jesus' name. Amen.

SCRIPTURE REFERENCES

Deuteronomy 26:1, 3 AMP   Hebrews 3:1 NCV

Ephesians 2:4-5 NCV

Deuteronomy 26:10-11, 14-15 NLT

Colossians 1:13 NLT

PART V:

A Godly Lifestyle

A Healthy Way of Life

FATHER, I am Your child, belonging only to You. Jesus is Lord over my spirit, soul, and body. Thank You for making me so wonderfully complex. Your workmanship is marvelous—how well I know it.

Lord, thank You for the plans You have for me—plans to prosper me and to give me hope and a future. I choose to renew my mind to Your plans for a healthy way of life. You have showered your kindness on me, along with all wisdom and understanding. I am sensible, and I watch my step. Continue to teach me knowledge and good judgment, for I trust Your commands.

My body is the temple of the Holy Spirit, who lives in me. So here is what I want to do with Your help, Father God. I choose to take my every day, ordinary life—my sleeping, eating, going-to-work, and walking-around life—and place it before You as an offering. Embracing what You do for me is the best thing I can do for You.

Christ, the Messiah, will be magnified and receive glory and praise in this body of mine and will be boldly exalted in my person. In Jesus' name. Amen.

SCRIPTURE REFERENCES

1 Thessalonians 5:23-24 NCV

Proverbs 14:15GW

Psalm 139:14 NLT

Psalm 119:66 NIV

Jeremiah 29:11 NIV

1 Corinthians 6:19 NLT

Romans 12:2 NIV

Romans 12:1MSG

Ephesians 1:8NLT

Philippians 1:20 AMP

Praising the Lord

Today and every day I will bless You, Lord, and Your praise will continually be in my mouth. I will say of You, Lord, that You are my refuge and strength and my portion forever. How lovely are Your dwelling places, my King and my God. I would rather have one day in Your courts than a thousand elsewhere. I am continuing to learn how to rest in Your precious presence and to say I hunger to be in Your courts.

Teach me to bring You praise from the rising of the sun to the going down of the same, for Your name is so worthy to be praised. Lord, who is like unto You? I say there is no one and nothing in all of creation that compares with You. I praise You for being compassionate, merciful, and full of benefits that You give to me each day.

Lord, every day I find something that causes my spirit to rejoice before Your presence. Even in times of testing and affliction, my soul can magnify You. Lord, I call You the King of Glory for You alone are eternal, immortal, invisible, the all-wise God who deserves honor and glory forever and ever. Amen.

SCRIPTURE REFERENCES

Psalm 34:1

Psalm 94:19 NIV

Psalm 68:19

Psalm 84:10

Psalm 113:3,4

Psalm 27:1

Exodus 34:6

1 Timothy 1:17

Time Alone with God

FATHER, I have come to spend time with You. I have learned to seek You early. I know that if I seek You early, I will find You. Before the call to things that will range from the mundane to levels of great importance, I need to satisfy my hunger for Your voice, Your counsel, and Your wisdom. I long for the joy of fellowship with You and the comfort it brings my soul.

This discipline of prayer gives me the opportunity to recount to You my concerns, hopes, fears, and desires. It is at this time, I am able to cast my cares [all my anxieties, all my worries, all my concerns, once for all] on You for You [care for me affectionately and care about me watchfully]. It affords me a place where I can sit with You and learn the rhythm of Your heart again. Our time together helps me see the larger picture of Your plans for my life. I can sit with You and talk as friend to friend. Be thou my vision forever1, I pray. Amen.

SCRIPTURE
REFERENCES

Psalm 63:1   1 Peter 5:7

Psalm 78:34   Psalm 5:2

Proverbs 8:17   Psalm 55:17

Peaceful Sleep

FATHER, thank You for peaceful sleep, and for Your angels that encamp around us who fear You. You deliver us and keep us safe. The angels excel in strength and heed the voice of Your Word. You give Your angels charge over me, to keep me in all my ways.

I bring every thought, every imagination, and every dream into the captivity and obedience of Jesus Christ. Father, I thank You that even as I sleep, my heart counsels me and reveals to me Your purpose and plan. Thank You for sweet sleep, for You promise Your beloved sweet sleep. My heart is glad, and my spirit rejoices while my body and soul rest, confidently dwelling in safety. Amen.

SCRIPTURE
REFERENCES

Psalms 16:7-9; 91:11; 103:20; 127:2

Matthew 16:19; 18:18   2 Corinthians 10:5

Proverbs 3:24

Protection

FATHER, You are my stronghold and my fortress. You are my God; in You will I trust. I will not be afraid of any terror by day or night, for You are always with me.

Lord, You are a shield about me to protect me. You are my light and my salvation—whom shall I fear? You are the stronghold of my life—of whom shall I be afraid? When evil men come to destroy me, they will stumble and fall!

I have peace in my heart because perfect love casts out all fear. You have not given me a spirit of fear, but of power and of love and of a sound mind.

Your Word promises me that no evil will come upon me, no accident will overtake me, and no disease or tragedy will come near my home. No weapon aimed at me will succeed. So I am strong, courageous, and fearless. Thank You for angels to keep me safe in all that I do.

Father, You have promised Your children a sweet, peaceful sleep, so I thank You that I can rest at night free from fear or nightmares. You give me peace and rest; Jesus is my safety.

Thank You for protecting me. In Jesus' name I pray. Amen.

To remind yourself of God's protection, read Psalm 91 and Psalm 23 often.

SCRIPTURE
REFERENCES

Psalms 3:3; 4:8; 23:4; 27:1,2; 91:5,9-12

Isaiah 54:17   2 Timothy 1:7

Psalm 34:7 AMP   1 John 3:8; 4:18

Maximizing Appearance

FATHER, Your Word says that You knitted me together in my mother's womb. My frame was not hidden from You when I was being formed in secret [and] intricately and curiously wrought [as if embroidered with various colors].

I know that Jesus came so I could enjoy life to its fullest. I speak Your words of life to myself. I will spend time developing a quiet and meek spirit. I know that my outward appearance is also important to You, for You care about every area of my life. You give me the desires of my heart when I delight myself in You and commit my ways to You.

I accept and feel good about myself, so that I am confident and present myself well. Help me to learn how to take care of myself and to maximize all the natural gifts that You gave me when You created me. Help me to listen to the Holy Spirit, the Teacher inside of me, keeping in mind that my body is His temple. I will control and discipline my body. I believe that with Your help, I can lose weight, or add and tone muscles, to maximize the physical beauty of the body that You gave me.

Father, help me to exercise consistently and take care of this temple of the Holy Spirit. Help me to be patient and to change any lifestyle or eating habits that might be destructive. Your Word is life to me and health to all my flesh.

I thank You for the beauty of a godly character. I treat my body with respect because Your Holy Spirit lives in me. I am so valuable that You gave Your only Son for my salvation. I believe that You are still perfecting everything that involves me, including the way I look. In Jesus' name I pray. Amen.

SCRIPTURE REFERENCES

Psalms 37:4,5; 100:3; 138:8; 149:4

Isaiah 44:2   John 3:16; 10:10

Psalm 139:13,15 AMP   1 Corinthians 6:19,20

Genesis 1:26,27, 31   1 Corinthians 9:25-27 AMP

Proverbs 4:20-22; 31:30   1 Peter 3:4; 5:7

Exercising Humility

ATHER, I choose to clothe myself in humility and to receive Your grace as I humble myself before Your mighty hand. I expect a life of victory and awesome deeds because my actions are done on behalf of a spirit humbly submitted to Your truth and righteousness.

Allow my thoughts and actions to be pure, just, and right. May I adjust my life so that I will know and understand the surety of Your plan for me.

Father, allow me to test my own actions, so that I can have appropriate self-esteem without comparing myself to somebody else. The security of Your guidance will allow me to carry my own load with energy and confidence.

I desire to listen carefully and hear what is being said to me. I incline my ear to wisdom and apply my heart to understanding and insight.

Father, I know and confess that humility and the fear of the Lord bring wealth and honor and life. Therefore, as one of Your chosen people, holy and dearly loved, I clothe myself with compassion, kindness, humility, gentleness, and patience. I bear with others and forgive whatever grievances I may have against anyone. I forgive as You forgave me. And over all these virtues I put on love, which binds them all together in perfect unity. I let the peace of Christ rule in my heart, and I am thankful.

Father, may Your will be done on earth in my life as it is in heaven. In Jesus' name I pray. Amen.

SCRIPTURE REFERENCES

1 Peter 5:5 NIV	Proverbs 2:2
Psalm 45:4 NIV	Proverbs 22:4 NIV
Galatians 6:4,5 NIV	Colossians 3:12-15 NIV
Proverbs 18:12,13 NIV	Matthew 6:10 NIV

Pleasing God Not Man

FATHER, I desire to please You rather than men. Forgive me for loving the approval and the praise and the glory that come from men [instead of and] more than the glory that comes from You. [I value my credit with You more than credit with men.]

I declare that I am free from the fear of man, which brings a snare. I lean on, trust in, and put my confidence in You. I am safe and set on high. I take comfort and am encouraged and confidently and boldly say, "The Lord is my Helper; I will not be seized with alarm [I will not fear or dread or be terrified]. What can man do to me?"

Just as You sent Jesus, You have sent me. You are ever with me, for I always seek to do what pleases You. In Jesus' name I pray. Amen.

SCRIPTURE
REFERENCES

John 12:43 AMP   John 17:18 AMP

Proverbs 29:25 AMP   John 8:29 AMP

Hebrews 13:6 AMP

Walking in God's Love

FATHER, I thank You that You have shown me through Your Word that the hallmark of my life as a believer is the love that I have for the brethren. I can walk in love because the Son of Your love dwells richly in me. I can love others because You have taught me to share the love You extend to me with everyone I meet.

I pray that every day I will walk in the fullness of the characteristics of love. For love is patient, kind, without envy, not boastful, and without pride. Your love in me is not rude, self-seeking, not easily angered, and refuses to keep a record of wrongs. Your love in me will not rejoice in evil but rejoices with the truth. This love always trusts, always hopes, and always perseveres. Your love in me will never fail.

Father, I ask that my love would abound more and more in knowledge and depth of insight, so that I may be able to discern what is best and to be pure and blameless until the day of Christ. I pray that I may model this love before others in a way that will cause them to see You anew and afresh. I pray that I will be an example of Your love in deeds, words, and behavior. I will dwell in Your love, and thereby, dwell continually in You. For we know that we have passed from death to life because we love the brethren.

I thank You, Lord God, that there is nothing that will be able to separate me from Your love. Nothing—not death, life, angels, demons, the present, the future, the past, powers of any kind, heights, depths, or anything in all of creation—will stop Your love from reaching me. I pray this in the name of Jesus. Amen.

SCRIPTURE REFERENCES

1 Corinthians 13   Philippians 1:9,10

Romans 8:38,39   1 John 4:12,16

1 John 3:14

Overcoming Temptation

FATHER, in the mighty name of Jesus, I come boldly to Your throne of grace that I may obtain mercy and find grace to help in my time of need. I ask forgiveness for rebelling against You and Your Word. I need Your deliverance and protection from every evil.

Lord, I want to be free from every form of evil, but I can't do it alone. I need Your help! I believe the truth of Your Word will set me free. Because Jesus has made me free, I am free indeed. When I am tempted, I ask You to show me the way of escape. Give me the grace I need to walk in the Spirit, so I won't fulfill the lusts of the flesh. Help me to control my thoughts.

Keep me from willful sins. May they not rule over me. Father, You are faithful. You will not allow me to be tempted beyond my powers of endurance. In every temptation You will always show me a way out. I determine not to go to the wrong types of parties or places that will make it easier to give in to alcohol/drugs/tobacco.

I will renew my mind by reading Your Word so that I can change the way I think and be set free from bad habits and from the lies that I have believed. I know that You will change my desires, Father, when I delight myself in You. Thank You that I have been freed from my sin by the blood of Jesus.

Thank You for forgiving me and for forgetting the sins of my past. I look to You for a great new future. It is a new day! I am a new person—I am a new creation in Christ Jesus.

Thank You, Lord, for a life free from rebellion and addictions. Please guide me to a godly counselor, friend, or support group. Thank You that You are giving me good habits where I once had bad habits. In Jesus' name I pray. Amen.

SCRIPTURE REFERENCES

Psalm 19:13; 37:4-6; 103:11-14

2 Timothy 4:18   Galatians 5:18-21

Hebrews 4:14-16   Romans 13:14

John 8:32,36   1 Corinthians 10:13

2 Peter 2:9 Phillips   1 Corinthians 15:33,34

Jeremiah 29:11   Isaiah 43:18,19

2 Corinthians 5:17

Living Holy

THANK You, Father, for making me holy by Your truth; You teach me Your Word, which is truth. Jesus, You gave Yourself as a holy sacrifice for me so I can be made holy by Your truth. Father, in Jesus' name, I confess my sins to You, and You are faithful and just to forgive me my sins and to cleanse me from all wickedness.

You live in me and walk with me—You are my God and I am Your child. So I leave the corruption and compromise; I leave it for good. You are my Father, and I will not link up with those who would pollute me, because You want me all for Yourself. I make myself pure—free from anything that makes body or soul unclean. I will try to become holy in the way I live because I respect You.

I throw off my old sinful nature and former way of life. I let the Spirit renew my thoughts and attitudes. I put on my new nature, created to be like You—truly righteous and holy. Lord, You made the way so I can have new life through Christ Jesus. Christ is my wisdom. Christ made me right with You. Now I am set apart for You and made holy. Christ bought me with His blood and made me free from sin.

I turn from evil and learn to do good, to seek justice, and help the oppressed. All who make themselves clean from evil will be used for noble purposes. I am made holy, useful to You, Master, and ready to do any good work.

Thank you, Lord, that I eat the best from the land, because You have given me a willing and obedient heart. Amen.

SCRIPTURE REFERENCES

John 17:17, 19 NLT	Ephesians 4:22-24 NLT
1 John 1:9 NLT	1 Corinthians 1:30 NLT
2 Corinthians 6:16 NCV	Isaiah 1:16-17 NLT
2 Corinthians 6:17 MSG	2 Timothy 2:21 NIV
2 Corinthians 7:1 NCV	Isaiah 1:19 GW

Health and Healing

FATHER, in the name of Jesus, I come before You asking You to heal me. It is written that the prayer of faith will save the sick, and the Lord will raise him up. And if I have committed sins, I will be forgiven. I let go of all unforgiveness, resentment, anger, and bad feelings toward anyone.

My body is the temple of the Holy Spirit, and I desire to be in good health. I seek that which will make me free—both spiritual (Your Word) and natural (good eating habits, medications if necessary, and appropriate rest and exercise). You bought me at a price, and I desire to glorify You in my spirit and my body—they both belong to You.

Thank You, Father, for sending Your Word to heal me and deliver me from all my destruction. Jesus, You are the Word who became flesh and dwelt among us. You bore my griefs (pains) and carried my sorrows (sickness). You were pierced through for my transgressions and crushed for my iniquities. The chastening for my well-being fell upon You and by Your scourging I am healed.

Father, I give attention to Your words and incline my ear to Your sayings. I will not let them depart from my sight but will keep them in the midst of my heart, for they are my life and health to my whole body.

Since the Spirit of Him who raised Jesus from the dead dwells in me, He who raised Christ from the dead will also give life to my mortal body through His Spirit, who dwells in me. Thank You that I will prosper and be in health, even as my soul prospers. Amen.

SCRIPTURE REFERENCES

James 5:15 NKJV

1 Corinthians 6:19-20

Psalm 107:20

John 1:14

Proverbs 4:21-22 NAS

Psalm 103:3-5 NAS

Romans 8:11 NKJV

3 John 2

Isaiah 53:4-5 NAS

When You Lose Something

ATHER, I come boldly to Your throne of grace in my time of need. I ask in the name of Jesus that You help me to find _____ (name the object that is lost). Thank You that You perfect that which concerns me. Holy Spirit, help me to remember where I was when I last saw or handled it.

Father, if I lost _____ due to my carelessness, please forgive me and help me to be more diligent in managing those things that You have so freely given me. I desire to make good use of everything I have.

You have blessed me with all spiritual blessings in Christ Jesus. Even the money I earn is a blessing from You. I commit the care of this situation to You, for I know that you care for me.

Because You are Lord over all of my life, Father, You will straighten my course and direct my feet. If someone deliberately took _____, I forgive that person and pray that the Holy Spirit will convince him/her of sin, of righteousness, and of judgment and will bring him/her to repentance.

Father, if You desire that I consider this loss as a gift, I do so in the name of Jesus and thank You for the return on it.

Thank You, Father, for guiding me and providing me with the answer. In Jesus' name I pray. Amen.

SCRIPTURE REFERENCES

Psalm 37:23

Psalm 73:24

Psalm 128:8 KJV

Proverbs 2:6-8

Proverbs 3:5-7 AMP

Proverbs 12:27 TLB

Proverbs 16:3

Ecclesiastes 5:19

Isaiah 30:21

Matthew 10:26

Luke 6:38

Luke 8:17

John 14:26

John 16:7,8 AMP

1 Corinthians 2:10

Ephesians 1:3

Hebrews 4:16

James 1:5

1 Peter 5:7 KJV

2 Peter 3:9 KJV

Glorify God

EAR Father, because of Your loving kindness to me, I worship You with my whole being. I offer you the gift of true worship. I know You are working in me, giving me the desire and the power to do what pleases You.

Father, since I am right with You, I will live by faith. I refuse to turn back with fear, for that would not please You. My body is the temple of the Holy Spirit who lives in me. I don't belong to myself. Lord, You bought me with a high price, and I honor You with my body.

I call on You in times of trouble; You save me, and I honor You. For you have rescued me from the dominion of darkness and brought me into the kingdom of the Son You love. With all my heart I will praise You, my Lord and my God. I will give glory to Your name forever!

I want You to say of me, "Well done, good and faithful servant." Thank You, Lord, for the gifts and talents You have given me. I will make good use of them and be a light for other people. I will live so they will see the good things I do give praise to You.

In Jesus' name, I will speak the truth in love, growing in every way more and more like Christ. Everything I say or do, I will do in the name of Jesus, giving thanks to You, God, my Father. In all the work I do, I will do the best I can. I will work as if I were doing it for You and not for people. Amen.

SCRIPTURE REFERENCES

Romans 12:1

Philippians 2:13

Hebrews 10:38b

1 Corinthians 6:20

Psalm 50:15

Colossians 1:13

Matthew 25:21

Romans 12:6

Matthew 5:16

Ephesians 4:15

Colossians 3:17

Colossians 3:23

Psalm 86:12

Tempted to Fear

FATHER, when I am afraid, I will trust in You. I praise You for Your Word. I trust you, God, so I resist fear and renounce fear of man. What can human beings do to me?

Thank You for giving me a spirit of power and of love and of a sound mind.

Because of this, I am not ashamed of the testimony of my Lord. I have not received a spirit that makes me a fearful slave. I acknowledge Your Spirit that I received when You adopted me as Your own child. Now, I can call you, "Abba Father."

Jesus, You rescued me by Your death. Because You embraced death and took it upon Yourself, You destroyed the devil's hold on death and freed me from cowering in life, being scared to death of death. I receive the gift that You gave me—peace! You give me Your own peace. This is not like when the people of the world say "peace" to me. You say it differently. You tell me not to fear and not to let anything trouble my heart. I receive this gift because I believe in You, God.

Lord, You are my light and the One who saves me. Why should I fear anyone? You protect my life from danger so why should I tremble? Evil people may try to destroy me. My enemies and those who hate me attack me, but they are defeated. Even if an army surrounds me, I will not be afraid. If I am attacked, I will trust in You, Lord.

Thank You, Holy Spirit, for bringing these things to my remembrance when I am tempted to be afraid. I will trust in my God. In the name of Jesus' I pray. Amen.

SCRIPTURE REFERENCES

Psalm 56:3 NCV

2 Timothy 1:7, 8 NKJV

Romans 8:15NLT

Hebrews 2:15 MSG

John 14:1,27 NLT

Psalm 27:1-3 NCV

PART VI:

Healthy Relationships

Love

FATHER, in Jesus name, I thank You that You fill my heart with love by the Holy Spirit which has been given to me. I keep and treasure Your Word. Your love and my love for You has truly reached its goal in me, and true love chases all my worries away.

Father, I am Your child, and I commit to walk in the God-kind of love. I will never give up. I care more for others than myself. I don't strut. I don't want what I don't have. I don't force myself on others or think about me first. I don't fly off the handle. I don't keep score of others' sins. I don't revel when others grovel, but I take pleasure in the flowering of truth. I put up with anything. I trust God always. I always look for the best, never looking back; I keep going until the end. The love of God in me never dies.

Father, I bless and pray for those who would harm me. I wish them well and do not curse them. Because of this, my love will overflow more and more in knowledge and understanding. I will live a pure and blameless life until the day of Christ's return. I am filled with the fruits of righteousness—the righteous character produced in my life by Christ Jesus.

Everywhere I go, I commit to plant seeds of love. I thank You, Father, for preparing hearts ahead of time to receive this love.

I know that these seeds will produce Your love in the hearts of those to whom they are given.

Father, I thank You that as I walk in Your love and wisdom, people are being blessed by my life. Father, You make me to find favor, respect, and affection with others (name them).

My life is strong and built on love. I know that You are on my side and nothing can separate me from Your love, Father, which is in Christ Jesus my Lord. Thank You, Father, in Jesus' precious name. Amen.

SCRIPTURE REFERENCES

Romans 5:5

Philippians 1:9-11 NLT

1 John 2:5 NCV

John 13:34

1 John 4:18 CEV

1 Corinthians 13:4-8 MSG

1 Corinthians 3:6

Daniel 1:9 NLT

Romans 12:14 NCV

Ephesians 3:17 NCV

Matthew 5:44

Romans 8:31,39

Choosing Godly Friends

FATHER, help me to show myself friendly and meet new friends. I want to spend time with wise people so that I may become wise by learning from them. I know that You are my source of love, companionship, and friendship. Help me to express and receive Your love and friendship with members of the body of Christ.

Just as iron sharpens iron, friends sharpen each other. As we learn from each other, may we share the same love and have one mind and purpose. Help me, Lord, to be well-balanced in my friendships so that I will always please You rather than others.

Lord, I ask for divine connections and good friendships and thank You for the courage and grace to let go of detrimental friendships. I ask for Your discernment for developing healthy relationships. Your Word says that two people are better than one because if one person falls, the other can reach out and help.

Father, only You know the hearts of people so help me to discern and not be deceived by outward appearances. Thank You, Lord, that every good and perfect gift comes from You, and I thank You for quality friends. Help me to be a friend to others and to love at all times. When others are happy, I will be happy with them. When they are sad, I will be sad with them. Help me to learn how to be a responsible and reliable friend.

Develop in me a fun personality and a good sense of humor. Help me to relax around people and be myself—the person You created me to be. I want to be a faithful and trustworthy friend to the people You are sending into my life. You are my help, Father, in my friendships.

Jesus is my best friend. He is a real friend who is more loyal than a brother. He defined the standard when He said in John 15:13 that there is no greater love than to lay down one's life for his friends.

Thank You, Lord, that I can trust You with myself and my need for friends. You are concerned with everything that concerns me. In Jesus' name. Amen.

SCRIPTURE REFERENCES

Proverbs 13:20 NIV

Ephesians 5:20 NIV

Philippians 2:2,3 NCV

Proverbs 13:20 NIV

Psalm 84:11 NIV

Ecclesiastes 4:9,10 NLT

1 Corinthians 15:33 CEV

James 1:17 NIV

Proverbs 17:17

Romans 12:15 CEV

Proverbs 18:24 NLT

Psalm 37:4,5 NCV

Proverbs 27:17 CEV

Home and Family

FATHER, I thank You that You have blessed me and my family with all spiritual blessings in Christ Jesus.

Through skillful and godly wisdom is my house (my life, my home, my family) built, and by understanding it is established [on a sound and good foundation]. And by knowledge shall its chambers [of every area] be filled with all precious and pleasant riches— great [priceless] treasure. The house of the [uncompromisingly] righteous shall stand. Prosperity and welfare are in my house, in the name of Jesus.

My house is securely built. It is founded on a rock—revelation knowledge of Your Word, Father. Jesus is its Cornerstone. Jesus is Lord of my household. Jesus is our Lord—spirit, soul, and body.

Whatever may be our task, we work at it heartily (from the soul), as [something done] for You, Lord, and not for men. We love each other with the God-kind of love, and we dwell in peace. Our home is committed to You [deposited into Your charge, entrusted to Your protection and care].

Father, I know not what others may do, but as for me and my house, we will serve the Lord. Hallelujah! In Jesus' name I pray. Amen.

SCRIPTURE REFERENCES

Ephesians 1:3

Proverbs 24:3,4 AMP

Proverbs 15:6 AMP

Proverbs 12:7

Psalm 112:3 AMP

Luke 6:48 AMP

Acts 16:31 AMP

Philippians 2:10,11 AMP

Colossians 3:23 AMP

Colossians 3:14,15 NIV

Acts 20:32 AMP

Joshua 24:15

Acts 4:11 AMP

Good Communication

FATHER, with all my heart I desire that my communication will continually be motivated by love for others. Show "me" to me so that I might change wrong attitudes and let go of prejudice and bad feelings toward others. Bring everything to the light. Expose insecurities that push me into being self-defensive; expose partisan bias that would exalt itself above Your purposes.

When anything is exposed and reproved by the light, it is made visible and clear, and where everything is visible and clear, there is light. Your light dispels the darkness, and I have no need for self-aggrandizement and self-promotion. I exchange my opinions for Your direction.

Teach me to guard my heart with all diligence, for out of it flow the very issues of life. I choose to speak the truth in love wherever I may be, in all my relationships. Thank You for giving me discernment as I listen to the ideas and opinions of others, especially when they are different than mine.

I will honestly esteem others and value their opinions, avoiding stupid and foolish controversies and dissensions and wrangling. The power of life and death is in the tongue, and You said that I would eat the fruit of it. A word out of my mouth may seem of no account, but it can accomplish nearly anything—or destroy it!

Father, forgive me for criticizing and judging others harshly. Forgive me for those times when I have knowingly or unknowingly twisted the truth to make myself sound wise. Sometimes my human anger was misdirected and worked unrighteousness. I thank You for forgiving me, and I forgive myself. You are cleansing me from all unrighteousness.

Father, I ask for wisdom from above and submit to the wisdom that begins with a holy life and is characterized by getting along with others. Use me as Your instrument in developing a God-fearing, healthy community. I will enjoy its results only if I do the hard work of getting along with others, treating them with dignity and honor. My tongue is as choice silver, and my lips feed and guide many. I open my mouth in skillful and godly wisdom to give counsel and clear instructions.

Lord, I love You with all my heart, and I will love others as well as I love myself. In the name of Jesus I pray. Amen.

SCRIPTURE
REFERENCES

1 John 3:1

Ephesians 4:29 NIV

Psalm 45:1 AMP

Proverbs 3:3 AMP

Proverbs 8:6-8 AMP

Proverbs 10:20,21 AMP

Proverbs 31:26 AMP

Romans 8:31-39 NIV

Hebrews 2:11 NIV

John 15:15 NIV

John 14:26

Titus 3:9

Matthew 6:6

Hebrews 11:6 AMP

Ephesians 5:13 AMP

Proverbs 4:23

Ephesians 4:15

Proverbs 18:21

James 3:5,6 MSG

James 3:9-16 MSG

James 3:17

James 3:17,18 MSG

Revelation 12:11

Preparing for Marriage

FATHER, sometimes being single can be so lonely and so painful. Seeing people in pairs, laughing and having fun, makes me feel even more alone and different.

Lord, please comfort me in these times. Help me to deal with my feelings and thoughts in an appropriate way. Help me to remember to work hard on myself so that I will be whole and mature when You bring the right person into my life.

Help me to remember that this is a time of preparation for the day when I will be joined to another human being for life. Show me how to be responsible for myself and how to allow others to be responsible for themselves.

Teach me about boundaries—what they are and how to establish them instead of walls. Teach me about love—Your love and how to say what is true and say it with love.

Father, I don't want to hold my future spouse or myself back. Help me to take a good look at myself and at who I am in Christ Jesus. Lead me to the right people—teachers, preachers, counselors, and to things—books, seminars, recordings—anyone and anything You can use to teach me Your ways of being and doing right.

Teach me how to choose the mate You would have for me. I ask You to make me wise and help me see things clearly. Help me to recognize the qualities You would have me look for in a mate.

Father, thank You for revealing to me that the choice of a mate is not to be based only on emotions and feelings, but You have definite guidelines in Your Word for me to use. I know that when I follow what You tell me to do, I will save myself and others a lot of pain and trouble.

Thank You, Lord, that You know me better than I know myself. You know my situation and You know the qualities that I need in another person to fulfill our destiny, individually and as a couple. I depend on You to protect me from the wrong people, so my plans will succeed. In Jesus' name I pray. Amen.

SCRIPTURE REFERENCES

1 Corinthians 1:3,4 NIV

Ephesians 4:15 WE

Matthew 6:33 AMP

James 1:5-8 WE

Proverbs 3:26 AMP

Proverbs 16:3 AMP

Never Alone

FATHER, when other people leave me and I feel unloved, I am thankful that You will never, ever leave me alone or reject me. You are a help for me in this time of loneliness. I know that Your angels are all around me.

You are my God. I know that You love me. Jesus even gave His life for me. I am a born-again Christian, Jesus lives in my heart, and I am on my way to heaven. That is plenty to be thankful for. So, I won't allow myself to be discouraged or feel sorry for myself. I choose to think only on those things that are pure, holy, and good, even when I am alone.

Although I may feel alone, I am not alone, for Your Word says that there is nothing that can separate me from the love of Christ. I will come out on top of every circumstance through Jesus' love. In Jesus' name I pray. Amen.

SCRIPTURE REFERENCES

John 16:32; 8:35,37; 10:9,10; 12:21

Psalms 34:7; 37:4; 46:1

Ephesians 4:31,32; 5:1,2

Deuteronomy 31:8   John 3:16; 16:32

1 Samuel 30:6   Philippians 4:8

Single Female
Trusting God for a Mate

FATHER, in the name of Jesus, I believe that You are at work in me, energizing and creating in me the power and desire to do Your will for Your good pleasure. You are preparing me to receive my future mate who will provide leadership to me the way You do to Your church, not by being domineering but by cherishing me.

Out of respect for Christ, we will be courteously reverent to one another.

Prepare me to understand and support my future husband in ways that show my support for You, the Christ.

Father, I believe because he has been divinely chosen by You, my future mate is full of Your wisdom which is straight-forward, gentle, reasonable, and overflowing with mercy and blessings. He speaks the truth in love.

Father, I believe that everything not of You shall be removed from my life. Forgive me for my past mistakes and heal the broken places. Your grace is sufficient as I prepare my heart to honor my future mate. Today, I purpose to always believe the best and to speak truly, live truly, and deal truly with marriage issues. I thank

You that every word that You give to me will come true. Father, I praise You for performing Your Word! Amen.

SCRIPTURE REFERENCES

Isaiah 62:5 NCV

Proverbs 8:8 NCV

Ephesians 5:25

Jeremiah 1:12MSG

James 3:17 MSG

Single Male
Trusting God for a Mate

FATHER, in the name of Jesus, I believe that You are providing a wonderful woman who will understand and support me. I pray that we will walk together with like faith and in agreement. Prepare me to provide leadership to my future wife the way You do to Your church, not by being domineering but by cherishing her.

Father, a wise wife is a gift from the Lord, and he who finds a wife finds what is good and receives favor from You.

Father, forgive me for my past sins and help me to always believe the best about my future wife. Teach me to be quick to listen and slow to speak. Father, I have written mercy and truth on the tablets of my heart and bind them about my mind. I will receive favor and good understanding from You and from others.

May Your will be done in my life, even as it is in heaven. Amen.

SCRIPTURE REFERENCES

Ephesians 5:22,23 MSG   Philippians 2:2 MSG

Proverbs 18:22NIV   Jeremiah 1:12 NLT

Proverbs 19:14

Fulfillment

FATHER, I thank You that I can steep my life into Your reality and Your provisions. I do not worry about missing out but know that my everyday human concerns will be met. I thank You that I know You love me, and I can trust Your Word.

Everything of You, Lord, gets expressed through Jesus so that I can see and hear You clearly. I don't need a telescope, a microscope, or a horoscope to realize the fullness of Christ and the emptiness of the universe without Him. When I come to You, that fullness comes together for me too. Your power extends over everything!

So, because of Jesus, I am complete, and Jesus is my Lord. I come before You, Father, thanking You that Your will be done in every area of my life. Now, I enter into Your rest by trusting in You. In the name of Jesus. Amen.

SCRIPTURE
REFERENCES

Matthew 6:33 MSG   Hebrews 4:10

Colossians 2:9,10 MSG

Boyfriend or Girlfriend Relationship

FATHER, I know that You care about every area of my life, especially who I date. So I thank You for a friend who knows You and is blessed with all spiritual blessings in Christ Jesus.

Thank You that we will develop a true friendship while we are maturing, learning from one another, and having fun.

Father, thank You for the Holy Spirit who reminds us to put You first while we develop a relationship that is pleasing to You. We will draw near to You, and You will draw near to us. We will resist the devil and he will flee from us.

Thank You for bringing us together so we can encourage each other and grow closer to You, Father. I pray that we will stay on fire for You and love Jesus more and more, so we can grow closer to You and minister to other people.

Knowing that unruly peers corrupt and destroy good morals, help us to use good judgment and say no when we are pressured to go places or behave contrary to Your will. I thank You for the Holy Spirit, who warns us of bad situations and leads us into good situations.

Father, help us be doers of the Word. Help us to treat each other with purity in our relationship, as brother and sister in the Lord. I pray that our relationship will be a healthy one, bringing growth and maturity to both of our lives. And thank You that we have favor and a good relationship with our families, because we know that this is important to You. Help us just to relax and develop our friendship.

Father, I pray that we will always listen to Your voice and be sensitive to Your Spirit so we don't set ourselves up for a fall. Help each of us establish sexual, physical, emotional, and intellectual boundaries so we may walk, live, and conduct ourselves in a manner worthy of You.

Thank You for Your angels who are protecting us from all harm, evil, or danger. Thank You for what You are doing in our lives. In Jesus' name I pray. Amen.

SCRIPTURE
REFERENCES

Psalms 37:4; 91:11   Ephesians 1:3

John 14:18   James 1:5,22

Romans 8:14   1 Peter 5:7

1 Corinthians 15:33 AMP

Committing to Purity

FATHER, I come before Your throne of grace in the name of Jesus. In the past I lived the way the world lives, doing all the things my body and mind wanted to do. But, God—Your mercy is great! Even though I was spiritually dead, You loved me so much that You gave me a new life with Christ. I have been saved by Your grace and raised up with Christ, seated with Him in the heavens.

You are my Father, and I belong to You. Since I am in Christ, I have become a new person. My old life is gone, and my new life has begun. Therefore, I rid myself of all malice, deceit, hypocrisy, envy, and slander of every kind. Like a newborn baby, I crave pure spiritual milk, so that I may grow up in Your salvation.

I submit myself to Jesus Christ, who loves me and sacrificed His life for me to make me holy, cleansing me through the baptism of His Word. I am now radiant in Your eyes—free from spot, wrinkle, and any other blemish. I am holy and without guilt.

Thank You for the blood of Christ that cleans me inside and out. Through the Spirit, Christ became an unblemished sacrifice for me, freeing me from all the dead-end efforts to make myself respectable so I can live all out for You! Thank You for giving me the Holy Spirit, who is holy and pure.

I ask for and receive wisdom, which comes from heaven—it is first of all pure; it is also peace loving, gentle at all times, willing to yield to others, full of mercy and good deeds, shows no favoritism, and is always sincere. Change my impure language, Lord, and give me clear and pure speech so it is pleasing to You.

I purpose not to conform to the ways of this world, but I am transformed by the renewing of my mind, and I take every thought captive to the obedience of Christ. I fix my thoughts on whatever is true, noble, right, pure, lovely, and admirable. I determine to think on things that are excellent or praiseworthy. I am careful what I think on, because thoughts run our lives.

What marvelous love You have extended to me, that I am now called and counted as a child of God! Father, I have no idea where I'll end up, but I do know that when You are openly revealed, I will see You and will become like You. Because of the blood of the Lamb and the word of my testimony, I will overcome. In Jesus' name I pray. Amen.

SCRIPTURE REFERENCES

Ephesians 2:2-6 NCV

2 Corinthians 5:17 NLT

1 Peter 2:1,2 NIV

Philippians 4:8 NIV

Proverbs 4:23 NCV

James 3:17 NLT

2 Corinthians 10:5 NASB

Ephesians 5:25-27 Phillips

Proverbs 15:16 NCV

Zephaniah 3:9 NLT

Romans 12:2 NIV

Hebrews 9:14 MSG

1 John 3:1-3 MSG

Revelation 12:11 NASB

Psalm 101:3 AMP

1 Thessalonians 4:8 NASB

When Someone Lies about You

FATHER, I come before You in the name of Jesus. Lies have been spoken against me, and I feel hurt, betrayed, and humiliated. I confess anger and hatred that I feel toward those who have spread these rumors. I know that Your Word says that I am to pray for those who persecute me, and that I am to love my enemies. These negative emotions keep getting in the way of my desire to obey Your Word.

I choose to give You these tormenting emotions that are robbing me of peace, love, joy, and sleep. Help me to release these agonies to You by forgiving those who have wronged me.

You and I know the truth, but the stares and whispers of former friends still hurt. I feel the cut off even from those who say they love me.

Jesus, You were shunned and forsaken by Your friends, and You understand the pain that I feel.

Father, I know that I cannot control the behavior of others, but with the help of the Holy Spirit, I can control mine. You said that no weapon formed against me will prevail and that every tongue that rises against me in judgment I shall show to be in the wrong.

I do believe that You keep me secretly in Your pavilion from the strife of tongues, from the lies that could cause me to behave in a spiteful and revengeful manner. You have given me the spirit of self-control, and I desire to walk before those who have hurt me in a manner that is pleasing to You, for You are the glory and the lifter of my head.

Lies endure for only a season, but truth endures forever. I thank You, Father, that You always cause me to triumph in Christ Jesus and that You have given me favor like a shield with all those who are involved. In Jesus' name I pray. Amen.

SCRIPTURE REFERENCES

Psalm 3:3 KJV

Psalm 5:12

Psalm 25:20,21

Psalm 26:1

Psalm 34:20 KJV

Psalm 37:1

Psalm 101:6-8

Proverbs 12:19 AMP

Proverbs 21:23

Isaiah 53:3

Isaiah 54:17 TLB

Matthew 5:44

Matthew 6:14,15

John 8:44

2 Corinthians 2:14 KJV

Ephesians 4:29

2 Timothy 1:7 AMP

James 1:19

PART VII:

The World Around Us

Helping Others

FATHER, in the name of Jesus, I will not withhold good from those who deserve it when it is in my power to help them. I will give to everyone what I owe them. I will pay my taxes and government fees to those who collect them, and I will give respect and honor to those who are in authority.

I will not become tired of helping others, for I will be rewarded when the time is right if I do not give up. So, right now, every time I get the chance, I will work for the benefit of all, starting with the people closest to me in the community of faith. Help me, Father, to be a blessing to all those around me.

I will not argue just to be arguing but will do my best to live at peace with everyone around me. Thank You, Father, for Your help in living this way. In the name of Jesus. Amen.

SCRIPTURE REFERENCES

Proverbs 3:27 NLT   Proverbs 3:30 CEV

Romans 13:7 NLT   Romans 12:18

Galatians 6:9,10 MSG

A Prayer for America

FATHER, in Jesus' name, we give thanks for the United States and its government. We pray and intercede for the leaders in our land: the president, the representatives, the senators, the judges, the governors, the mayors, the police officers, and all those in authority over us in any way. We pray that the Spirit of the Lord rests upon them.

We believe that skillful and godly wisdom has entered into the heart of our president and knowledge is pleasant to him. Discretion watches over him; understanding keeps him and delivers him from evil.

Father, we ask that You encircle the president with people who make their hearts and ears attentive to godly counsel and do right in Your sight. We believe You cause the people of our American government to be people of integrity who are obedient concerning us, so that we may lead a quiet and peaceable life in all godliness and honesty. We pray that the upright shall dwell in our government—that leaders blameless and complete in Your sight shall remain but the wicked shall be cut off and the treacherous rooted out.

Your Word declares that "blessed is the nation whose God is the Lord" (Ps. 33:12). We receive Your blessing. Father, You are our refuge and stronghold in times of trouble (high cost, destitution, and desperation). So we declare with our mouths that Your people dwell safely in this land, and we prosper abundantly. We are more than conquerors through Christ Jesus!

It is written in Your Word that the heart of the king is in the hand of the Lord, and You turn it whichever way You desire. We believe the heart of our leader is in Your hand and that his decisions are directed of the Lord.

We give thanks unto You that the good news of the gospel is published in our land. The Word of the Lord prevails and grows mightily in the hearts and lives of the people. Thanks for this land and the leaders You have given to us, in Jesus' name. Jesus is Lord over the United States! Amen.

SCRIPTURE
REFERENCES

1 Timothy 2:1-3   Deuteronomy 28:10,11

Proverbs 2:10-12,21,22; 21:1

Romans 8:37 AMP   Acts 12:24

Psalms 9:9; 33:12

Prayer for a Person Who Needs Salvation

FATHER, in the name of Jesus, I make a joyful noise to the Lord and serve You with gladness! I come before You with singing! I know that You are God!

It is written in Your Word that Jesus came to seek and save the lost. You wish all people to be saved and to know Your divine truth. Therefore, Father, I bring _____ before You this day.

Thank You for calling me to be Your agent of intercession for _____ . By the grace of God, I will build up the wall and stand in the gap before You for _____ , that he/she might be spared from eternal destruction.

Father, thank You for salvation. I acknowledge Jesus as the Lamb of God, who takes away a person's sins, and the Holy Spirit, who convicts and convinces him/her of sin, righteousness, and judgment. Your kindness leads _____ to repent (to change his/her mind and inner man to accept Your will). You are the One who delivers _____ and draws him/her to Yourself out of the control and the dominion of darkness and transfers him/her into the kingdom of the Son of Your love.

Father, I pray that _____ will hear the truth from someone standing in Your presence. The Good News was hidden from _____ . Satan, the god of this world, made him/her blind, and he/she was unable to see the glorious light of the gospel. Now, I ask You, Lord of the harvest, to thrust the perfect laborer into _____ 's path to share Your gospel in a special way so that he/she will listen and understand it. As Your laborer ministers to him/her, I believe that he/she will come to his/her senses—come out of the snare of the devil who has held him/her captive—and make Jesus the Lord of his/her life.

Having prayed all that I know to pray, I submit to the Spirit, who also helps me in my present limitations. I do not always know how to pray worthily, but Your Spirit within me is actually praying for me in those agonizing longings which cannot find words.

Having done all to stand, I stand on Your Word, and Father, I shall praise You and thank You for _____ 's salvation. I commit this matter into Your hands, and with my faith I see _____ saved and filled with Your Spirit, with a full and clear knowledge of Your Word. Amen—so be it!

SCRIPTURE REFERENCES

Psalm 100:1-3 AMP

Colossians 1:13 AMP

Luke 19:10

2 Corinthians 4:2-4 TLB

2 Peter 3:9

Matthew 9:38 AMP

2 Timothy 2:26 NIV

John 1:29

Romans 8:26 Phillips

John 16:8-12 AMP

Ephesians 6:13

Romans 2:4 AMP

Ezekiel 22:30 AMP

Note to Reader: When you are praying for an individual's salvation, it is necessary that you allow patience to have her perfect work. Stand against discouragement, doubt, and unbelief by enforcing the victory Jesus won at Calvary. The Lord is your confidence, and your prayer must be founded on the faithfulness of God. Ask forgiveness when you are doubtful or distrustful and continue fighting the "good fight of faith."

In your intercession, you will be up against a stronghold of independence, which separates mankind from God. Inappropriate independence reinforces self-conceit: "No one will tell me what to do."

Those who are lost cannot discern the truth. If the eyes of their heart are to be flooded with light so that they can know and understand truth, the veil of pride must be removed.

Satan cannot control the mind of the unbeliever, but he does influence his/her thinking. Your prayers initiate mind-liberation when you engage God's mighty weapons to knock down the devil's strongholds—proud arguments against God. You can knock down walls that keep men from finding Him. (Read 2 Corinthians 4 and Ephesians 1:18).

Maintain your prayer armor and wield the sword of the Spirit, which is the Word of God (Eph. 6:10-18).

Proclaim aloud: With God's mighty weapons, I can capture and bring him/her back to God and influence _____ into being a man/woman whose heart's desire is obedience to Christ (2 Cor. 10:3-6 TLB). I will not give up, but I will pray until _____ receives a revelation—the lifting of the veil.

Praise: I rejoice because the counsel of hell shall not prevail against _____ 's salvation. Thank You, Father, that the illuminating light of the knowledge of the glory of God is revealed to _____ . You are bringing him/her to repentance by your goodness, and he/she will receive a new knowledge that will replace his/her arrogant thinking. Amen.

Satan, you have no choice. _____ is protected by the blood of Jesus. _____ is no longer under your authority but he/she now belongs to Jesus!

* After you have prayed this prayer, thank the Lord for this person's salvation. Rejoice and praise God for the victory! Confess the above prayer as done! Thank the Lord for sending the right laborer. Thank Him that Satan is defeated. Hallelujah!

Prayer for a Person Who Needs Favor

FATHER, in the name of Jesus, You smile on _____ and are gracious and kind to him/her. He/she is the head and not the tail, above and not underneath.

Thank You for favor for _____ who seeks first Your kingdom and finds delight in good. Grace (favor) is with _____ who loves the Lord Jesus with an undying love. He/she gives favor, honor, and love to others, and You pour out on him/her a spirit of favor until his/her cup runs over. Crown him/her with glory and honor because he/she is Your masterpiece, which has been created new in Christ Jesus. He/she is strong, wise, and blessed by You.

Give _____ knowledge and skill in all learning and wisdom. Cause him/her to find favor, compassion, and loving-kindness with _____ (names). _____ finds favor in the sight of all who look upon him/her this day, in the name of Jesus.

I pray that _____ knows the love of Christ and is filled up with the fullness of God. You are doing far more beyond all that _____ asks or thinks, because Your mighty power

PRAYERS that avail much. for Graduates

is at work in him/her. Thank You, Father, that _____ is well-favored by You and by man, in Jesus' name. Amen.

SCRIPTURE REFERENCES

Numbers 6:25 NLT

Deuteronomy 28:13 NASB

Matthew 6:33 NCV

Proverbs 11:27 MSG

Ephesians 6:24 NIV

Luke 6:38 WE

Zechariah 12:10 NIV

Psalm 8:5 NCV

Ephesians 2:10 NLT

Luke 2:40 WE

Daniel 1:17 AMP

Daniel 1:9 AMP

Esther 2:15,17 NLT

Ephesians 3;19-20 NASB

Prayer for a Person Who Needs Protection

FATHER, in the name of Jesus, I lift up _____ to you and pray a hedge of protection around him/her. I thank You, Father, that You are a wall of fire around about _____ and that You have sent Your angels to encamp around about him/her.

I thank You, Father, that _____ dwells in the secret place of the Most High and abides under the shadow of the Almighty. I say of You, Lord, that You are his/her refuge and fortress, his/her God. In You will he/she trust. You cover _____ with Your feathers and under Your wings shall he/she trust. Your truth shall be his/her shield and buckler.

_____ shall not be afraid of the terror by night, nor of the arrow that flies by day. Only with his/her eyes will he/she behold and see the reward of the wicked.

Because _____ has made You, Lord, his/her refuge and habitation, no evil shall befall him/her—no accident will overtake him/her—neither shall any plague or calamity come near him/her. For You will give Your angels charge over him/her, to keep him/her in all Your ways.

Father, because _____ has set his/her love upon You, therefore will You deliver him/her. He/she shall call upon You, and You will answer him/her.

You will be with _____ in trouble; You will deliver him/her and will satisfy him/her with long life and show him/her Your salvation. In Jesus' name I pray. Amen.

SCRIPTURE REFERENCES

Job 1:10	Psalm 91:4,5
Zechariah 2:5	Psalm 91:8-11
Psalm 34:7	Psalm 91:14-16
Psalm 91:1,2	

Prayer for a Person Who Needs a Job

FATHER, in Jesus' name, I believe and confess Your Word over _____ today, knowing that you watch over Your Word to perform it. Your Word prospers in _____, to whom it is sent!

Father, You are _____'s source of every comfort (consolation and encouragement). He/she is courageous and grows in strength.

_____'s desire is to owe no man anything except to love him. Therefore, he/she is strong and does not let his/her hands be weak and slack, for his/her work shall be rewarded. His/her wages are not counted as a favor or a gift but as an obligation (something owed to him/her).

_____ makes it his/her ambition and definitely endeavors to live quietly and peacefully, to mind his/her own affairs and to work with his/her hands. He/she is correct and honorable and commands the respect of the outside world, being dependent on nobody[self-supporting], and having need of nothing, for You, Father, supply (fill to the full) his/her every need.

_____ works in quietness and earns his/her own food and other necessities. He/she is not weary of doing right [but continues in well-doing without weakening].

He/she learns to apply himself/herself to good deeds (to honest labor and honorable employment) so that he/she is able to meet necessary demands whenever the occasion may require.

Father, You know [the record of] _____ 's works and what he/she is doing. You have set before him/her a door wide open, which no one is able to shut.

_____ does not fear and is not dismayed, for you, Father, strengthen him/her. You help him/her, in Jesus' name. In Jesus, _____ has [perfect] peace and confidence and is of good cheer, because Jesus overcame the world and deprived it of its power to harm. _____ does not fret or have anxiety about anything, for Your peace, Father, mounts guard over his/her heart and mind.

_____ knows the secret of facing every situation, [for he/she is self-sufficient in Christ's sufficiency]. He/she guards his/her mouth and his/her tongue, keeping himself/herself from trouble.

_____ prizes Your wisdom, Father, and acknowledges You. You direct and make straight and plain his/her path, and You promote him/her.

Therefore, Father, _____ increases in Your wisdom (in broad and full understanding) and in stature and years and in favor with You and man! In Jesus' name I pray. Amen.

SCRIPTURE REFERENCES

Jeremiah 1:12 AMP

Isaiah 55:11 AMP

1 Corinthians 1:3 AMP

1 Corinthians 16:13 AMP

Romans 13:8 AMP

2 Chronicles 15:7 AMP

Romans 4:4 AMP

Titus 3:14 AMP

Revelation 3:8 AMP

Isaiah 41:10 AMP

John 16:33 AMP

Philippians 4:6,7 AMP

Philippians 4:12,13 AMP

Proverbs 21:23 AMP

1 Thessalonians 4:11,12 AMP

Proverbs 3:6 AMP

Philippians 4:19 AMP

Proverbs 4:8 AMP

2 Thessalonians 3:12,13 AMP

Luke 2:52 AMP

Prayer for a Person Experiencing Grief or Loss

FATHER, in the name of Jesus, I approach Your throne of grace, bringing _____ before You. I recognize that grieving is a human emotional process, and I give him/her the space that he/she needs to enter in to the rest that You have for him/her.

Lord, Jesus bore _____ 's griefs (sicknesses, weaknesses, and distresses) and carried his/her sorrows and pains. I know Your Spirit is upon Jesus to bind up and heal _____ 's broken heart. May he/she be gentle with himself/herself, knowing that he/she is not alone in grief. You are with him/her, and You will never leave him/her without support.

Father, I desire to be a doer of Your Word, and not a hearer only. Therefore, I make a commitment to rejoice with those who rejoice [sharing others' joy], and to weep with those who weep [sharing others' grief]. I pray that my love will give _____ great joy and comfort and encouragement, because he/she has refreshed the hearts of Your people.

Thank You, Father, for sending the Holy Spirit to comfort, counsel, help, intercede for, defend, strengthen, and stand by _____ in this time of grief and sorrow. In Jesus' name I pray. Amen.

SCRIPTURE REFERENCES

Isaiah 53:4 AMP

Isaiah 61:1 AMP

Hebrews 13:5 AMP

2 Corinthians 12:9 Phillips

Galatians 6:2 Phillips

James 1:22

Romans 12:15 AMP

Galatians 6:2 AMP

Philemon 7 AMP

John 14:26

Ephesians 4:2 AMP

Boldness to Witness

FATHER, in the name of Jesus, I ask You to give me the courage to speak Your Word with great boldness. When the Holy Spirit came upon me, I received the power to be Your witness. I will tell people about You everywhere. Thank You for giving me this wonderful message of reconciliation that You are no longer counting people's sins against them. I pray for right words to speak so I can make known the mystery of the gospel for which I am an ambassador of Jesus Christ. God, You make Your appeal through me, and I speak for You when I plead, "Come back to God!"

I take comfort and am encouraged and confidently and boldly say, "The Lord is my Helper! I will not be seized with alarm—I will not fear or dread or be terrified. What can man do to me?" Father God, You made Christ, who never sinned, to be the offering for my sin so that I am made right with You through Christ. I am complete in Him, righteous and as bold as a lion. In Jesus' name. Amen.

SCRIPTURE REFERENCES

1 Corinthians 5:19-21 NLT

Hebrews 13:6 AMP

Protection for My Family

FATHER, in the name of Jesus, I lift up my family to You and pray a wall of protection around us—our home and property. Father, You are a wall of fire around us, and You have sent Your angels to protect us.

I thank You that we live under the protection of God Most High and stay in the shadow of God All-Powerful. We will say to You, Lord, that You are our fortress, our place of safety. You are our God, and we trust You! You will cover us with Your feathers and hide us under Your wings. We will not fear any danger by night or an arrow during the day. We will watch and see the sinful punished.

You are our fortress, and we run to You for safety. Because of this, no terrible disasters will strike us or our home. You will command Your angels to protects us wherever we go. You have said in Your Word that You will save whomever loves You. You will protect those who know You. You will be with us in trouble. You will rescue us and honor us and give us a long, full life and show us Your salvation. Not a hair of our head will perish.

Thank You, Father, for Your watch, care, and protection over my family and me. In Jesus' name. Amen.

SCRIPTURE REFERENCES

Job 1:10 NLT

Zechariah 2:5

Psalm 34:7 CEV

Psalm 91:1,2 CEV

Psalm 91:8 NCV

Psalm 9:9-11 CEV

Psalm 91:14-16 NCV

Luke 21:18 NIV

Psalm 91:4,5 NCV

Living in a Polarized World of Darkness and Light

FATHER God, thank You for loving me and preparing me for such a time as this. Jesus is my Lord and as He is so am I in this world.

I choose not to be obsessed with getting my own advantage. I choose to forget myself long enough to lend a helping hand and walk in love while surrounded by a world of darkness. Christ and I are one; You are in me, testing and probing my every motive. You are working everything together to accomplish Your purpose as I seek to fulfill my mission in a world of darkness and outrage.

I choose to live as Your masterpiece re-created in Christ Jesus and avoid evil by worshiping Jehovah. The power of Your faithful love removes sin's guilt and grip over me. I am working in a world of instant gratification and listening to people of other cultures and backgrounds who have walked where I've never walked.

You have given me the mind of Christ, and I bring my thoughts into alignment with Your thoughts. Your kingdom revelations will break open my understanding and unveil the deeper meaning of riddles. I choose to cling to Your words and receive discipline to demonstrate wisdom in all my relationships.

God, You will never give me the *spirit of* fear, but the Holy *Spirit* who gives me mighty power, *love*, and self-control. I am going out into the world uncorrupted, a breath of fresh air in this squalid and polluted society. Father, use me to provide people with a glimpse of good living and of the living God.

I am carrying the light-giving Message into the night. In the name of Jesus. Amen.

SCRIPTURE REFERENCES

Philippians 2:1-8, 14-16 MSG

Proverbs 16 TPT   Proverbs 1 TPT

Ephesians 2:10 NLT   1 Timothy 1:7 TPT

Your Life Makes A Difference in the World

Throughout your life you will find yourself returning again and again to this book of prayers. Prayer is conversing with God, the Creator of the universe, on an intimate level. You love Him because He first loved you. You are here for such a time as this—you can change your generation!

Everybody has a story. Your story will be completed as you fulfill your God-given destiny. Regardless of your career choice—maintain a practice of prayer. Learn to be a team player and always remain teachable. Determine to be ever learning, growing, and achieving. You make a difference! You have influence!

God needs you functioning in your ability. The spiritual infrastructure of our society must be rebuilt, and we need people of understanding and insight who will go into the marketplaces and make a difference. God may lead you into government, education, economy, religion, arts and entertainment, and family! Be the best you and influence your world.

Embrace godly wisdom. "Wise people are builders—they build families, businesses, communities. And through intelligence and insight their enterprises are established and endure. Because of their skilled leadership the hearts of people are filled with the treasures of wisdom and the pleasures of spiritual wealthy" (Proverbs 24:3-4 TPT).

Take a realistic view of the world we live in today and ask God where you are to rebuild and bring heaven to earth. Your gift will make room for you and bring transformation to your workplace, your city, your church, and your nation.

Unite with others in prayer and keep a prayer journal of prayer needs and answered prayer.

You are writing your story.

Receiving Jesus
as Lord and Savior

(The most important prayer of all!)

F ATHER, it is written in Your Word that if I confess with my mouth that Jesus is Lord and believe in my heart that You have raised Him from the dead, I shall be saved.

Therefore, Father, I confess that Jesus is my Lord. I make Him Lord of my life right now. I believe in my heart that You raised Jesus from the dead. I renounce my past life with Satan and close the door to any of his devices.

I thank You for forgiving me of all my sin. Jesus is my Lord, and I am a new creation. Old things have passed away; now all things become new in Jesus' name. Amen.

If you prayed the prayer to receive Jesus as Savior and Lord for the first time, please contact us at www.harrisonhouse.com. We want to share your good news and bless you with a free book. Or you may write to us at

Harrison House
P.O. Box 310
Shippensburg, Pennsylvania 17257-0310

SCRIPTURE REFERENCES

John 3:16

John 6:37

John l0:l0

Romans 3:23

1 Corinthians 5:19

John 16:8,9

Romans 5:8

John 14:6

Romans 10:9,10

Romans 10:13

Ephesians 2:1-10

2 Corinthians 5:17

John 1:12

2 Corinthians 5:21

Prayer to Receive the Infilling of the Holy Spirit

M Y heavenly Father, I am Your child, for I believe in my heart that Jesus has been raised from the dead, and I have confessed Him as my Lord.

Jesus said, "How much more shall your heavenly Father give the Holy Spirit to those who ask Him." I ask You now in the name of Jesus to fill me with the Holy Spirit. I step into the fullness and power that I desire in the name of Jesus. I confess that I am a Spirit-filled Christian. As I yield my vocal organs by faith to You, my Lord, I expect to speak spirit to spirit as the Spirit gives utterance. Praise the Lord! Amen.

SCRIPTURE REFERENCES

John 14:16,17

Luke 11:13

Acts 1:8

Acts 2:4

Acts 2:32,33,39

Acts 8:12-17

Acts 19:2,5,6

Romans 10:9,10

1 Corinthians14:2-15

1 Corinthians 14:18,27

Ephesians 6:18

Jude 1:20

Acts 10:44-46

About the Author

GERMAINE COPELAND had a visitation from God on the day she had planned her suicide. From that time, she talked with God and He talked to her through the pages of the Bible. God, the Father, Jesus, and the Holy Spirit were real! Germaine asked the Holy Spirit to teach her to pray effectively. She wrote Scriptures as prayers for her family and her son's deliverance from a lifestyle of addictions. Over that twenty-eight-year period, God taught her and she taught others the dynamics and discipline of prayer. Her books series, *Prayers That Avail Much,*° has changed the lives of people around the world. She is the Founder of Prayers That Avail Much (formerly known as Word Ministries, Inc.) and her son, David Copeland, is Vice-President of the ministry. She and her husband, Everette Donald Copeland, reside in Greensboro, Georgia. Together, they pray for their four children, grandchildren, great grandchildren, and future generations.

Mission Statement

Word Ministries, Inc.

To motivate individuals to spiritual growth and emotional wholeness, encouraging them to become more deeply and intimately acquainted with the Father God as they pray prayers that avail much.

You may contact Word Ministries by writing
Word Ministries, Inc.
P. O. Box 289 Good Hope, GA 30642
770-267-7603
www.prayers.org

Please include your testimonies
and praise reports when you write.

Other Books by Germaine Copeland

A Global Call to Prayer

Prayers That Avail Much Commemorative Gift Edition
burgundy leather

Prayers That Avail Much
gold-letter gift edition

Prayers That Avail Much
gold-letter paperback

Prayers That Avail Much 25th Edition
hardback

Prayers That Avail Much Commemorative
paperback

Prayers That Avail Much Devotional

Prayers That Avail Much for Grandparents

Prayers That Avail Much for Leaders

Prayers That Avail Much for the New Believer
mini book

Prayers That Avail Much for Parents
mini book

Prayers That Avail Much for Young Adults

Prayers That Avail Much for the Workplace

365 Days to A Prayer-Filled Life

Prayers That Avail Much for America

Prayers That Avail Much for the Nations

Harrison House

REACH US AT:
1-800-722-6774

The Harrison House Vision

Proclaiming the truth and the power
of the Gospel of Jesus Christ with excellence.
Challenging Christians
to live victoriously,
grow spiritually,
know God intimately.